P9-DMP-481

THE HEBREW PROPHETS

THE CLASSIC BIBLE BOOKS SERIES

The Song of Solomon: Love Poetry of the Spirit
Introduced and Edited by Lawrence Boadt;
Foreword by John Updike

The Hebrew Prophets: Visionaries of the Ancient World
Introduced and Edited by Lawrence Boadt;
Foreword by Desmond Tutu

The Great Sayings of Jesus: Proverbs, Parables and Prayers
Introduced and Edited by John Drane;
Foreword by Richard Holloway

The Gospel of St John: The Story of the Son of God
Introduced and Edited by John Drane;
Foreword by Piers Paul Read

Forthcoming

The Book of Job: Why Do the Innocent Suffer?
Introduced and Edited by Lawrence Boadt;
Foreword by Alice Thomas Ellis

Genesis: The Book of Beginnings
Introduced and Edited by Lawrence Boadt;
Foreword by Sara Maitland

The Psalms: Ancient Poetry of the Spirit
Introduced and Edited by Lawrence Boadt and F. F. Bruce;
Foreword by R. S. Thomas

Sayings of the Wise: The Legacy of King Solomon
Introduced and Edited by Lawrence Boadt;
Foreword by Libby Purves

Stories from the Old Testament: Volume I
Introduced and Edited by Lawrence Boadt;
Foreword by Monica Furlong

Stories from the Old Testament: Volume II
Introduced and Edited by Lawrence Boadt;
Foreword by Morris West

The New Testament Epistles: Early Christian Wisdom
Introduced and Edited by John Drane;
Foreword by Roger McGough

Revelation: The Apocalypse of St John
Introduced and Edited by John Drane;
Foreword by Richard Harries

THE HEBREW PROPHETS
Visionaries of the Ancient World

INTRODUCED AND EDITED BY LAWRENCE BOADT
FOREWORD BY DESMOND TUTU

St. Martin's Griffin
New York

THE HEBREW PROPHETS: VISIONARIES OF THE ANCIENT WORLD
Copyright © Lion Publishing, 1997. All rights reserved. Printed in the
United States of America. No part of this book may be used or repro-
duced in any manner whatsoever without written permission except in
the case of brief quotations embodied in critical articles or reviews. For
information, address St. Martin's Press, 175 Fifth Avenue,
New York, N.Y. 10010.

ISBN 0-312-22210-6 cloth
ISBN 0-312-22076-6 paperback

Library of Congress Cataloging-in-Publication Data
is available from the Library of Congress.

First published in Great Britain by Lion Publishing plc, 1997.
First St. Martin's Griffin edition: June 1999
10 9 8 7 6 5 4 3 2 1

Contents

Foreword

Some people have thought that the prophets of Israel were a band of soothsayers, something like the Delphic oracles of ancient Greece. They would then be the sort of person one would consult if one hoped to win the lottery. But the prophets were nothing of the sort. They were not glorified crystal ball gazers whose chief activity was to predict the future. Sometimes it has been said that they were much more 'forth-tellers' than 'fore-tellers', because they were fundamentally God's spokespersons. They characteristically proclaimed, 'Thus saith the Lord…'. They brought a message from the Lord whose mouthpiece they claimed to be. Aaron was designated to speak on behalf of the ineloquent Moses, and the Lord then said that Aaron would be like a prophet and Moses would be like his deity.

They were inspired to speak for God, but not as if God were playing on them as a musician plays on an inanimate violin, as some of the early Fathers suggested. They were not just scribes taking down divine dictation and adding nothing to that divine message. No, God spoke through them as they were, the medium of communicating God's message. The Word of God came through the words of real men and women, not just robots. They mediated that Word through their personalities, through their circumstances, through their gifts and weaknesses. So an Isaiah, with a heightened sense of God's holiness, sees the Lord high and lifted up and is overwhelmed by his own sinfulness and impurity; or a Hosea, through his heartrending experience of marital infidelity, sees it all as a reflection of the relationship between an unfaithful Israel and a patient and mercifully loving God-husband.

The prophets spoke into a particular situation in the present – declaring the demands and will of God in the here and now. 'Thus saith the Lord…' to this king, to these people of Israel who were the prophet's contemporaries. Almost always they sought to recall the people of Israel to what they knew about their God's dealings with his people in the past as providing a clue to his character and so to his will and demands for them in the present. They were trying to move their fellow Israelites on the basis of their common tradition to obey God, to urge them to trust him who had proved so trustworthy in the past and not to place their trust in the false gods they were so frequently tempted to worship. Nor should they have a superstitious faith in an apparently inviolate Zion or its temple and elaborate worship, for these were unacceptable substitutes. Failure to have such undivided loyalty to God or obedience to his decrees was bound to have the most dire consequences. It is these consequences that the prophets predicted as inevitable, given the moral nature of the God whose spokespersons they claimed to be.

But this God was not ultimately wrathful. His intention for Israel and so for all creation was beneficent. God desired the best for all his creatures and so the prophets saw in their poetic imagination, as artists see, the new world God wanted to bring into being. Like poets they used highly emotive and richly imaginative language to describe this new world and the good time coming. In places, their descriptions were reminiscent of the idyllic time of the beginning described in Genesis, when universal harmony reigned, when the lamb lay down with the lion. Hermann Gunkel described this as *Endzeit ist Urzeit* – 'endtime is as beginning time'.

The will of their God was that Israel should live in an exemplary manner – where the widow, the orphan and the alien were cared for as of infinite worth; where justice would flow like a river; where goodness would root out evil; where the strong cared for the weak; where the hungry were fed; where prisoners were set free; where the blind were made to see, the deaf to hear, the lame whole again, the dumb to speak – all these not as optional extras but as of the essence of religion. They had to love God and their neighbour as themselves, otherwise it was all an abomination.

How anyone having read the prophets could say, 'Do not mix religion with politics' is quite baffling. Which Bible had they read? 'Religion is about the whole of life' is what the prophets were proclaiming. In situations of injustice nothing could be so revolutionary and so subversive of that *status quo* than the Bible and its prophets. Thanks be to God. They inspired us in our struggle against apartheid. We have won a great victory for peace and reconciliation, goodness and mercy.

May they always remain such a potent source of inspiration.

Desmond Tutu

INTRODUCTION

The Rise of Prophecy

Although 1 and 2 Kings are the first major sources in the Bible to mention large numbers of prophets active throughout the two kingdoms of Judah and Israel, it is not the first notice of prophetic activity among the chosen people. Already in Numbers 23–24, a pagan prophet Balaam is hired to curse Israel, and instead offers oracles of blessing. Samuel, the great leader of the last days of the judges, is interpreted as a prophet in what he does. Prophecy also played a role in the life of King David. He had two court prophets, Nathan and Gad, who offered divine guidance and sometimes condemnation in matters of royal policy. Even the events from the time of the conquest in the books of Joshua and Judges are presented by the authors as responses to divine words. In fact, the prophetic word is made to play such an important role in all these books that Jewish tradition refers to them simply as the 'Former Prophets' (Joshua, Judges, 1 and 2 Samuel and 1 and 2 Kings), as distinguished from the 'Latter Prophets', whose collected oracles have come down to us in books under their individual names (Isaiah, Hosea, Jeremiah, etc.).

The first of these 'Latter Prophets', Amos, marks a turning point in our knowledge of prophecy. Up to his time – the middle of the eighth century BC – all our knowledge of prophecy depends on stories *about* the prophets. From Amos on, we can examine and study their actual words and the contributions they made to Israel's faith. In comparison to the rich words that they have left us, the information on earlier prophets, even an Elijah or Elisha, seems very scanty and often coloured by imaginative details and folk-tale heroism.

Prophecy itself used to be considered a unique characteristic of Israel not found elsewhere in the ancient world. But that view prevailed when the Bible was our only source of knowledge of the ancient world. Since the last century, new information about prophecy in other nations has come to light as a result of archaeological digging. Babylonian and Assyrian records speak of a large class of vaguely 'prophetic' persons associated with temples.

Most of these sought the will of the gods through divination, that is, reading unusual signs in natural objects. Since it was difficult to know what the gods wanted human leaders to do, experts would interpret extraordinary 'divine' signs such as the movement of the stars, or deformities in the livers of sheep, or the flight of a flock of birds, or the meaning of dreams. It was through these unusual signals, all free from human tampering or 'fixing', that the gods could indicate what decisions should be taken. Divination was a highly technical job and the Babylonian priests have left many clay tablets of instructions on how to interpret such things as sheep livers. But beyond this type of seeking God's word, it was also recognized that God might speak directly to individuals in dreams or trances. In the Atrahasis epic, a version of the Babylonian flood story, the god Enki speaks to the hero in sleep. In letters of the eighteenth century BC found in the great Babylonian city of Mari (located on the Euphrates River) numerous prophets and prophetesses send oracles to their king, Zimri-Lim, to communicate special commands from the gods. Usually these were given in a trance in a temple setting, and copied down by the priest and sent on to the king along with a piece of the speaker's hair and clothes, to make sure that the person was not lying. One such oracle reads:

> Speak to my lord: Thus Mukannishum your servant, I offered a sacrifice to Dagan for the life of my lord, and then the *aplum* (prophet) of Dagan of Tuttul arose and spoke as follows: 'O Babylon! How must you be constantly treated? I am going to gather you into a net... I will deliver in to the power of Zimri-Lim the houses of the seven confederates and all their possessions.'(ANET 625)

Here the local priest is performing the daily sacrifice on behalf of the king's welfare, when a prophetic person is inspired to deliver an oracle against the enemy state of Babylon which predicts a victory for Mari's ruler over the Babylonian confederation. Many of these pagan prophets seem to be part of the official priesthood of temples, but others, especially the ecstatics, were ordinary people with special gifts of clairvoyance or other psychic powers.

In the Bible itself, the earliest mention of prophetic roles comes in the form of divinations to discover the divine will. The story of Gideon in Judges 6 tells how Gideon requested a sign from God by letting his fleece remain dry overnight while the ground nearby was covered with dew. The Books of Samuel mention the *urim* and *thummin* as a means of asking God for a yes or no answer on several occasions (1 Samuel 14:18, 36–37, 41; 23:10–13). Apparently they were a white and a black ball, and drawing a white ball meant 'yes'. This was a formal way to 'seek Yahweh's will' (Judges 1:1–2; 1 Samuel 10:22–23), and, according to directions in Exodus 28, was reserved to the high priest.

More strictly prophetic is the story of Balaam in Numbers 22–24. The King of Moab hires a famous 'seer' to curse Israel. Balaam offers sacrifices, has a vision and speaks words that come from outside himself. Unfortunately for the king of Moab, the prophet utters blessings instead of curses on Israel. The text explicitly says in Numbers 23:5 that 'God puts a word in Balaam's mouth'. He does not speak his own thoughts but becomes a mouthpiece for God. In Numbers 24 the text of the oldest oracles goes on to suggest that this word came in the form of a visionary trance:

> The oracle of Balam, son of Beor,
>   the oracle of the one whose eye is opened,
> The oracle of one who hears God's words
>   and sees a vision of the almighty,
>   swooning but with his eye uncovered.
> (Numbers 24:15–16)

This is the classic definition of a 'seer' whose prophetic insight comes through some sort of 'third eye' vision accompanied by words. It perfectly describes the talents of Samuel to find lost objects and see distant events in 1 Samuel 9:5–20, and of Elisha with his 'vision' of men coming to visit him in 2 Kings 6:32, his prediction that the king will die in 2 Kings 8:10, and his vision of his servant Gehazi afar off in 2 Kings 5:26.

Closely related to this older form of prophecy are the so-called 'sons of the prophets' that occur in the period from Samuel down to Elisha, about 200 years in all. These are bands of prophets who follow a leader such as Elisha, who is called the 'father' of the group. They travel about and often use musical instruments to initiate a trance-like state. This is said to be the 'spirit of God' rushing upon them, and is wonderfully described in two events from Saul's life in which he meets a band of such 'sons of the prophets' and goes into a trance, rolling on the ground, stripping off his clothes, and becoming 'another man' (1 Samuel 10:5–12; 19:23–24).

The Writing Prophets

The classical prophets after the time of Amos still use the term 'spirit of God' to describe their source of prophetic messages. See, for example, Ezekiel's vision of the dry bones in Ezekiel 37. The call of Isaiah to be a prophet in Isaiah 6 clearly resembles a trance-like state. But what is surprising is how rarely such language occurs among the great writing prophets. Most of their oracles are introduced by the very simple statement: 'The word of the Lord came to me', or just 'Thus says the Lord.' We cannot be sure how this word came, whether in a trance or a dream (as it did to the earlier Nathan in 2 Samuel 7), or whether in some sudden insight or overwhelming inspiration under more normal circumstances.

The word that they use of themselves, *nabi* (in Hebrew), means 'one called' or 'one who is called'. The title indicates that the person does not speak his or her own words, but the words of God. Our English word for the *nabi*, 'prophet', is derived from the Greek term *prop-phates*, 'one who speaks on behalf of another', that is, a herald or announcer. It thus means the same. There are a number of indications within the Old Testament that this conviction that the words they spoke came directly from God was based on the prophetic experience of being summoned in some kind of a vision to hear God speak to the *heavenly throne room*. The charming story of the prophet Micaiah ben Imlah in 1 Kings 22 pits this single Yahweh prophet against hundreds of false prophets who only tell the king what he wants to hear. Micaiah claims that he is better than they because he has actually stood in heaven and heard what God was going to do. Jeremiah says the same in Jeremiah 23, and Isaiah's vision in Isaiah 6 presupposes that the prophet is looking in to the heavenly throne room. The prophet participates in the decisions made by God and his angelic advisors.

The best description of this whole heavenly courtroom can be found in the opening chapters of the Book of Job where Satan and God carry on their dialogue over the fate of the hero.

We must be careful when comparing early and late prophecy because it is always possible that the editors and writers of the Old Testament described early prophecy in terms of how Israel experienced the later prophecy of their own times when men like Isaiah and Jeremiah were preaching their messages. But it certainly seems safe to conclude that early forms of prophecy in Israel leaned more to the discovery of the divine will for specific occasions and for specific individuals. The prophetic personnel were marked by great psychic gifts of seeing the future and by powers of divination. Some of these prophets were members of organized groups that favoured ecstatic behaviour rather than 'messages' to be delivered, and many were part of the payroll of kings or temples and could be called on for a vision or prediction in moments of need. This role contrasts sharply with the concerns of the writing prophets who speak to the whole nation and who see their primary task as challenging popular but false values while exhorting the people to rediscover the covenant and to reverse their evil ways. But both types have in common the concern to speak for those without a voice, that is, the underprivileged and forgotten, the poor and the victims of injustice. They also share a strong sense of the tradition of the covenant which looks upon all Israelites as sharers in the blessings of the Lord and thus entitled to be treated with justice. Because of this standpoint, which puts them outside the power centres and allows them to criticize Israel's kings and leaders as well as the common people, the prophets contributed a powerful new factor to Israel's idea of itself, namely the conviction that they are not God's people unless they are *morally* upright. From the prophets on, Israel considers the *ethical* dimension to be as important as the *worship* of Yahweh's name in cult.

Collecting and Editing the Prophet's Words

With the appearance of Amos, we enter the period of Israel's history that is usually called 'Classical Prophecy'. It gets this name because the writings left by individual prophets became the standard for interpreting Israel's faith by both later Jews and Christians. When trying to capture the spirit of the prophet's thought, readers often assume that every word comes from the prophet himself. Yet the titles of books under individual names such as Amos or Hosea do not imply that they contain just the words of Amos and Hosea, but also words *about*, and in the *tradition of*, the prophet. Nor are the oracles and sayings necessarily in the logical or chronological order that we would like. Ancient editors have collected and arranged words spoken by these prophets in an order that seemed important to them but often escapes us. Editors frequently added words taken from disciples of the prophet, or even unknown prophetic words that are similar in theme and which add to the thought of the prophet in whose book they are included. Even more dramatically, later generations who cherished the words of an Amos or Micah occasionally added new application and comments from their own centuries to the collected words of the long-dead prophet. This was a natural development. Each prophet had faced a specific need in his day, whether it was a certain king's greed or the attack of an Assyrian army or whatever. When kings were no more and Assyrians had long ago became notes in history books, Israel still read the words of the prophets as inspired guides for a new age, but they needed to show that those words now applied to life in exile or without a temple and royal family. It is much the same as when Christians apply the meaning of Jesus' gospel to problems that never existed in his own time: nuclear war, abortion, test tube babies and others.

The most notable example of this process of editing and expanding the thought of a prophet can be seen in the book of Isaiah. Careful scholarship has identified three separate collections of oracles, and perhaps more, joined together as one book. Each collection has its own special style and references to dates and events that makes its historical setting in life different from the other two parts. The first and most important grouping is from the great prophet Isaiah himself, found in chapters 1–39, and includes oracles and words that he spoke plus several later oracles, such as chapters 24–27.

A second major section is found in chapters 40–55. These chapters speak of Babylon rather than Assyria, and hope for a Persian liberator,

Cyrus, to come and free Israel from exile. The author uses a distinctive style which mixes hymns of praise with courtroom lawsuits. Whoever this great genius was, he lived some 200 years after the original Isaiah, and carried the earlier message of trust in a holy God who loved Zion to a terrible new age of exile and total loss of Zion which Israel suffered under the Babylonians in 586BC.

The last major division, Isaiah 56–66, makes still a third collection, spoken and kept in the years after Israel was freed from exile by the Persian king, Cyrus the Great, in 539 and had returned to the ruined and desperately poor homeland of Judah. It has a much more sombre and penitential mood than Second Isaiah, but at times it also moves to moments of great hope and a vision of the restored glory at Zion that will someday come about, more typical of First Isaiah's message.

We can learn much by paying attention to the different levels in a prophetic book. It helps to understand how God's people heard the oracles of a prophet, kept them, saw new meanings in them as the years went by, and constantly reminded themselves that God's word did not die but lived anew for each generation just as powerfully as when the prophet had first spoken it. Because of this living force of the divine speech, different levels are never seen as different and separated messages, but form a single book where each part helps the reader understand the other parts in a larger vision of history. It creates a dynamic forward motion of the word through time. Proof of the importance of this union of different parts into one whole can easily be seen in the fact that both Jews and Christians have traditionally understood the prophets as messengers of God's promise and hope, predictors of future restoration, even though most of the words are judgment and damnation and warnings of destruction. Why is this? Because a combination of words from several periods of time reveals not a single final judgment, but a record of God's mercy which returns again and again to speak to Israel in new ways.

Lawrence Boadt

THE HEBREW PROPHETS IN LITERATURE

Quotations and Images

Quotations and Images

Ancient of Days

Daniel 7:7–22 describes an apocalyptic night-vision of Daniel in which 'the books' are opened before the Ancient of Days, 'whose garment was as white as snow, and the hair of his head like the pure wool: his throne was like the fiery flame, and his wheels as burning fire' (v. 9). This scene of judgment climaxes with an approach to the throne by 'one like the Son of man' (v. 13), unto whom is then given 'dominion, and glory, and a kingdom... which shall not pass away' (v. 14). The title 'Ancient of Days' alternates in the passage with 'Most High' (vv. 18–27) and seems to indicate God enthroned in judgment over world empires. In Aramaic *attiq yomin* means 'advanced in days' and corresponds to a similar description of Zeus in hellenic art and literature. The term is cited throughout talmudic literature and becomes 'the head of days' in 1 Enoch 46. Rashi identifies the figure with God, other sources with an angel. St Augustine typifies patristic exegesis in seeing the Ancient of Days as God the Father, and adds that Daniel's vision provides a concrete example of the Father's appearing to the prophets in bodily form, so that 'it is not, therefore, unsuitably believed that God the Father was also wont to appear in that manner to mortals' (*De Trinitate*, 18.33).

John Donne, in his 'La Corona' sonnet, asks the 'all changing unchang'd Antient of dayes' to receive his collection of sonnets as a 'crown of prayer and praise'. The most famous evocation of the Ancient of Days in English literary history, however, may well be Blake's frontispiece illustration for *Europe*, in which he is also a *deus pancreator*, constricted, as Blake would see it, by the limitations of mathematical form (rpt. M. Klonsky, *William Blake*, 1977, 40). For Coleridge, 'to contemplate the ancient of days and all his works with feelings as fresh as if all had then sprung forth at the first creative fiat characterizes the mind that feels the riddle of the world, and may help to unravel it' (*Biographia Literaria*, chapter 3; cf. Byron, *Childe Harold's Pilgrimage*, 2.2.1).

David L. Jeffrey
University of Ottawa

Babylon

In the Old Testament *Babylon* is a magnificent, sinful, pagan, and prideful city-state upon the Euphrates in the land of Chaldea (Shinar). Genesis 10:8–10 mentions the founding of Babylon, or Babel, by the 'mighty hunter' Nimrod, and in Genesis 11:1–9 the proud Babylonians are building their 'tower, whose top may reach the heavens'. The second book of Kings 24–25 chronicles the wars of Babylon's Nebuchadnezzar upon Israel, wars which resulted first in Jerusalem's subjugation and the exile to Babylon of its leading citizens (whence the so-called 'Babylonian exile' of the popes to Avignon, 1307–77), and ultimately in Jerusalem's destruction.

The wars with mighty Babylon are at the heart of repeated condemnations of the city by Jeremiah, Isaiah, and Ezekiel, and of their prophecies of its catastrophic demise and Jerusalem's deliverance. Isaiah prophesies that 'Babylon, the glory of kingdoms... shall be as when God overthrew Sodom and Gomorrah' (Isaiah 13:19; cf. 21:1–10). Jeremiah is equally vivid: Babylon 'shall become heaps, a dwelling place for dragons, an astonishment and a hissing, without an inhabitant' (Jeremiah 51:37; cf. chapters 50–51).

Where Babylon is mentioned in the New Testament, Rome, the 'new Babylon', is usually intended. Certainly this interpretation was a commonplace from St Victorinus to the marginal glosses of the Geneva Bible. Babylon could also be used to stand for earthly power and moral decadence in the last days. For John, Babylon is 'the great whore' (Revelation 19:2), a city in which merchants peddle 'gold, and silver... and chariots, and slaves, and souls of men' (18:10–13). This Babylon will be cast down and utterly destroyed in the last days (18).

For St Augustine the Babylonian captivity is 'our captivity', Israel's deliverance 'our deliverance'. Jerusalem and Babylon are to be contrasted, the 'vision of peace' versus 'confusion'. (For Augustine, this contrast was rooted in the etymology of their respective names; the popular meaning of Babel, and hence for Babylon – sanctioned in Genesis 11:9 – was accepted generally; cf. St Isidore of Seville, *Etymologiae*, 15.1.4.) Augustine associates the two cities with two loves – the love of God, or charity, with Jerusalem and the love of the world, cupidity, with Babylon. Drawing on the experience of the captive Hebrews, he argues that one can be a true citizen of Jerusalem even while a captive sojourning in Babylon (cf. *De civitate Dei*, esp. bk. 14). Rabanus Maurus (*Patrologia Latina*, 112.872) elaborates this typology, providing a whole set of allegorical equivalences: Babylon is the 'evil city' and so Jeremiah 51:6 ('flee out of the midst of Babylon') can be taken to mean 'condemn and forsake immorality'; Babylon can represent hell, the world, the impious, sin, and even, recalling 1 Peter 5:13, the Gentile church. In his commentary on Ezekiel 3:10–11, St Gregory says that the journey from Jerusalem to Babylon is the soul's descent from righteousness to evil (*Homiliarum in Ezechielem*, *Patrologia Latina*, 76.894).

These traditions are carried over into English literature. In the Middle English poem *Cleanness* Babylon is an exemplum of pride and worldly grandeur brought low, while after the Reformation Babylon was an oft-hurled barb in sectarian debate: 'By Babylon we understand the church of Rome,' says Richard Hooker confidently (*Sermons*, 2.10), reflecting a well-established connection (cf. Luther's *Babylonian Captivity of the Church*). Had his allegiances been otherwise, he might, along with certain Puritans, have understood the Church of England. David Austin's *Downfall of Mystical Babylon* (1794) is an American variation, in which the author of *The Rod of Moses upon the Rock of Calvary* (1816) attempts to establish connections between Protestant typology and Masonic symbolism.

In less polemical contexts Babylon is frequently recalled as a place of wealth (Chaucer, *Book of the Duchess*, 1061), worldly renown (Pope, 'Temple of Fame', 64), and sin (Herbert, 'Church Militant', 103). F. Scott Fitzgerald's 'Babylon Revisited' makes use of a wide range of these traditions: his protagonist Charlie has left America, with its work ethic and related values, to go to Paris to live the gaudy life in the years before the stock market crash of 1929. There he squanders his wealth, his wife, and his daughter. In remorseful memory, Charlie's return to Paris, now depression Paris, Babylon after its fall, is also a return to his Babylonian state of mind. The power of Babylon figuratively to entrap its habitual denizens is well illustrated by Jorge Luis Borges' short story 'The Lottery in Babylon', a dispassionate narration of life in a Dantean hell of random fortune and terror.

H. David Brumble
University of Pittsburgh

Bruised Reed

King Hezekiah had been warned not to trust Egypt, 'the staff of this bruised reed... on which if a man lean' it will break and pierce his hand (2 Kings 18:21; Isaiah 36:6); but of the Lord's chosen Isaiah later wrote, 'A bruised reed shall he not break, and the smoking flax shall he not quench: he shall bring forth judgment unto truth' (42:3). This latter verse was quoted by Jesus (Matthew 12:20).

The expression is developed especially in Protestant commentary as an encouragement to perseverance in faith and repentant hope. Matthew Poole's *Annotations upon the Holy Bible* (Matthew 12:20) interprets the passage as saying that 'He will not discourage those that are weak in Faith, or weak in Hope,' and sees the smoking flax as an 'apt Metaphor to express such as believe, but are full of Doubts and Fears, or such as have a Truth of Grace, but yet much Corruption'.

George Herbert makes a graceful liturgical use of the allusion in 'The Banquet':

> But as Pomanders and wood
>   Still are good,
> Yet being bruis'd are better sented:
> God, to show how farre his love
>   Could improve,
> Here, as broken, is presented. (25–30)

In Shakespeare's *2 Henry 6* (1.2.1; 24–27) Duke Humphrey's wife describes him in his dispirited state: 'Why droops my lord, like overripened corn, / hanging the head...', and he answers concerning his troubling dream, 'Methought this staff, mine office badge in Court / Was broke in twain' – as he imagines, by the Cardinal. Edward Young, in his *Night Thoughts*, urges his reader to 'Lean not on Earth, 'twill pierce thee to the heart; / a broken reed at best'; Longfellow, in his sonnet to Keats, would rewrite the dead poet's epitaph: 'The smoking flax before it burst to flame / Was quenched by death, and broken the bruised reed.' In commending 'The Eternal Goodness' Whittier writes 'The bruised reed he will not break / But strengthen and sustain,' but the phrase is often applied to human relationships, as when Holmes says to Watson in Arthur Conan Doyle's 'The

Adventure of the Three Gables' (*The Case-Book of Sherlock Holmes*), 'I made a mistake, I fear, in not asking you to spend the night on guard. This fellow has clearly proved a broken reed.' In Dickens' *Little Dorrit* old Dorrit says of poor Nandy: 'I do – ha – extend as much protection and kindness to the – hum – bruised reed – I trust I may call him so without impropriety – as in my circumstances, I can,' a satiric and intentionally damning use of the allusion.

David L. Jeffrey
University of Ottawa

Dry Bones, Valley of

In Ezekiel 37 the prophet describes being 'carried out in the spirit of the Lord' and set down 'in the midst of the valley which was full of [human] bones' (v. 1), which were very dry. The Spirit asked him, 'Son of man, can these bones live?' to which Ezekiel replied, 'O Lord God, thou knowest.' Ezekiel was then instructed to prophesy upon the bones, commanding them to 'hear the word of the LORD' (v. 4). God declared that he would cause the bones to be reknit, sinews and flesh laid upon them, and their skin to return, by his 'breath' (*ruah*); immediately the earth shook and the bones were enfleshed. Ezekiel was then told to say, 'Come from the four winds, O breath, and breathe upon these slain, that they may live' (v. 9). When the four winds came rushing together into the valley the corpses arose and came to life as 'an exceeding great army' (v. 10). In the text itself the vision is interpreted as an allegory of the restoration of defeated Israel and its return to its own land (vv. 11–14).

With the exception of Ezekiel's initial vision of the Shekinah glory of God in its mystical chariot, 'wheels within wheels', this is the most influential passage in Ezekiel's prophecy. The liturgical use of Ezekiel 37:1–14 is ancient, providing the *hapthard* for Passover and its Sabbath, corresponding there to the Sidroth (Exodus 33:12 – 34:26 and Numbers 28:19–25). It appears in early temple art on the lower frieze of the north wall at the Synagogue of Dura-Europos (3rd century AD), which interprets the resurrection of the dead in literal terms as an eschatological promise, not as an image for the restoration of Israel. The resurrected souls appear here with wings. This interpretation is not, however, shared by many other Jewish sources. R. Eliezer says that one should understand that immediately after the resurrected individuals stood up, they died (Sanhedrin 92b). Other targums say the dead were Ephraimites, or that they went up to Palestine, married, and had children (e.g., Diéz-Macho, *Targum Palestinense*, 201). In a lighter vein, the Talmud tells how Nebuchadnezzar learned of the resurrection of the dry bones: he had a drinking cup made of the skull and bones of a slain Jew. When he lifted it to drink, the bones came swiftly to life and then punched the Babylonian king in the face as a voice declared: 'A friend of this man is at this moment reviving the dead!' (Sanhedrin 93a). Another midrash tells how the resurrected men wept because they feared that, having been once resurrected, they would lose their share in the life to come: Ezekiel is said to have reassured them on this count (Pirqe de Rabbi Eliezer, 33).

In Christian tradition the Fathers (e.g., St Irenaeus, Tertullian, St Justin Martyr, St Cyprian, St Cyril of Jerusalem, and St John of Damascus) tended to see the episode as a prefiguration of the final resurrection. St Ambrose writes: 'Great is the loving kindness of the Lord, that the prophet is taken as a witness of the future resurrection, that we, too, might see it with his eyes' (*De excessu fratris satyri*, 2.73; cf. *De Spiritu Sancto*, 3.19.149). In the services of the Church the passage was associated with Lent and Easter, and in all Latin rites it formed one of the lections for the baptism of catechumens on Easter Eve; as St Jerome says, it was *in omnium ecclesiarum Christi lectione celebrata*.

Perhaps the most whimsical use in English literature, saving Du Bose Heyward's 'Roll dem bones,' is Izaak Walton's record of John Donne's melodramatically preaching his own funeral sermon, so ill that 'many did secretly ask that question in Ezekiel: "Do these bones live?"'(*Life of Dr John Donne*). Dryden, following the early tradition, connects the whole passage to the Resurrection and Last Judgment:

> When in mid-aire, the Golden Trump shall sound,
> To raise the Nations under ground;
> When in the Valley of Jehosaphat,
> The Judging God shall close the Book of Fate...

> When rattling Bones together fly,
> From the four Corners of the Skie,
> When Sinews o'er the Skeletons are spread...
> The Sacred Poets first shall hear the Sound,
> And foremost from the Tomb shall bound.
> ('To the Pious Memory of... Anne Kiligrew,' 178–89)

In *Benito Cereno* Melville describes a neglected whaleboat as looking like it must have been 'launched, from Ezekiel's Valley of Dry Bones'. Whittier, in 'Howard at Atlanta', describes a group of slaves reading the Bible together, in a scene perhaps proleptic of the famous spiritual:

> Behold! – the dumb lips speaking,
> The blind eyes seeing!
> Bones of the Prophet's vision
> Warmed into being!

Daniel Sargent's 'The Last Day' calls up the army of bones for a battle to end all battles, seeing the ghostly army as set for Armageddon.

David L. Jeffrey
University of Ottawa

Flesh is Grass

The opening passage of the second part of the book of Isaiah, 'Comfort ye my people', made memorable to millions in the English-speaking world through Handel's *Messiah*, continues with the reminder: 'All flesh is grass, and all the goodliness thereof is as the flower of the field: The grass withereth, the flower fadeth: because the spirit of the Lord bloweth upon it: surely the people is grass. The grass withereth, the flower fadeth: but the word of our God shall stand forever' (Isaiah 40:6–8). The image of human life as grass, eventually to be mowed down for hay, is found throughout the Psalms (e.g., 37:2; 102:4, 11; 103:15), in Job (5:25), and in 1 Peter (2:24–25, where the apostle is citing the Isaiah passage).

The text receives straightforward commentary from the Fathers. St Augustine is representative when he observes, reflecting on Psalm

103: 'The whole splendour of the human race; honour, powers, riches, pride, threats – is the flower of the grass. That house flourishes, this family is great, that family prospers, but how many years do they live? Many years to you are but a short season to God. God does not count as you do' (*Enarrationes in Psalmos* 103.19, on v. 15). Death is a kind of harvest, as of hay, or a winnowing of the grain from the chaff, the chaff then being 'for the fire' (*Enarrationes in Psalmos* 52.8, on v. 6; cf. 60.2). In this sense, he says, even 'grass bearing fruit, as is that of wheat... is called "grass" in Holy Scripture' (72.18). The contrast between perishable grass and the durable Word of God is, for Augustine, another reason to marvel at the incarnation:

> Inasmuch then as he knows as a father our forming, that we are but grass, and can only flourish for a time, he sent unto us his Word, and his Word, which abides for evermore, he has made a brother unto the grass which does not last long. Do not wonder that you shall be a sharer in his eternity then; he became first himself a sharer in your condition as grass... How great then is the hope of the grass, since the Word has been made flesh? That which lives forever has not disdained to assume the lot of grass, that grass might not despair of itself. (*Enarrationes in Psalmos*, 103.19–20; on vv. 15–16)

Because of its recurrence in the Psalms and Job as well as Isaiah, the phrase was well worked in medieval preaching and in spiritual literature. An interesting reflection of the image in painting of the 16th century is provided by the 'Haywain Triptych' of Hieronymus Bosch, an altarpiece which, when folded, shows a harried pilgrim; when the panels are opened the story of Creation and Fall is represented on the left, while in the centre a host of secular and ecclesiastical persons frantically pursue a large wagon-load of hay (or chaff, really – straw) into the fiery hell depicted on the right. The connection of the phrase with life's pilgrimage persists in poetry as well. Donne writes ('To Sr. Henry Wotton'): 'But I should wither in one day, and passe / To "a bottle" of Hay, that am a locke of Grasse. / Life is a voyage...' In Herbert's 'Miserie', the poet observes, 'Man is but grasse, / He knows it, fill the glasse.' In his poem 'Frailtie' he builds upon Augustine's commentary (*Enarrationes in Psalmos*, 103.21), as well as the text:

Lord, in my silence how do I despise
    What upon trust
Is styled *honour, riches*, or *fair eyes;*
    But is *fair dust!*
    I surname them *guilded clay,*
  Dear earth, fine grasse, or *hay.*

In later literature the phrase is a cliché whose biblical origin is nevertheless usually recognized. Byron deals in *Don Juan* with the inevitability of death as Cheops' mummy is confronted, but to a different conclusion: 'And "flesh" (which Death mows down to hay) "is grass"; / You've passed your youth not so unpleasantly' (1.1756–57). Elizabeth Gaskell illustrates one type of 19th-century adaptation in 'The Old Nurse's Story': '"Flesh is grass", they do say; but who would have thought that Miss Furnivall had been such an out-and-out beauty, to see her now?' Similarly, in Shaw's *Back to Methuselah* the phrase signifies merely the fading potency of elderly life. When Zoo reproaches the Elderly Gentleman for being apparently proud of his age, he says, 'What does it matter to you whether anything is true or not? Your flesh is as grass: you come up like a flower, and wither in your second childhood. A lie will last your time: it will not last mine' (4.1; cf. Job 14:2). P.G. Wodehouse makes light-hearted use of the phrase in several of his novels and stories: 'We are all sorry that the Reverend Whatever-he-was-called should be dying of adenoids, but after all, here today, gone tomorrow, and all flesh is grass, and what not…' (*Right Ho, Jeeves*, chapter 17; cf. *The Adventures of Sally*, 8.3; 'Romance at Droitgate Spa').

David L. Jeffrey
University of Ottawa

Four Beasts

In a vision of Daniel (7:3–8), 'four great beasts came up from the sea… The first was like a lion, and had eagle's wings.' The second was 'like to a bear', the third 'like a leopard' – with four wings and four heads – the fourth was 'dreadful and terrible, and strong exceedingly; and it had great iron teeth… and it had ten horns'. It is generally agreed that these beasts symbolized four kingdoms, each of which ruled Israel in its turn, although which of the kingdoms corresponds to which of the beasts has long been a subject of debate. For St Jerome (*Commentarii in Danielem*) and St Augustine (*De civitate Dei*, 20.23), Assyria, Persia, Macedonia, and Rome were the appropriate designates. The beast of Revelation 13:1–10, which John saw 'rise up out of the sea... like unto a leopard, [with]... the feet of a bear... the mouth of a lion', and the power of a 'dragon', is apparently a composite of Daniel's four beasts and seems for John to have stood for worldly government in general and/or Roman government in particular. The Glossa Ordinaria interprets it synthetically as 'Antichristus, vel generaliter tota collectio malorum' (*Patrologia Latina*, 114.733).

In medieval and Renaissance English literature the beasts come to be more simply associated with the devil and evil – especially in apocalyptic contexts – as in Spenser's borrowing of 'Three ranckes of yron teeth' with which the Redcrosse Knight's dragon is endowed (*Faerie Queene*, 1.11.13), although the two-horned composite creature of Revelation 13:11–18 is adopted as 'the Ram' by David Jones in a parodic passage in his *The Sleeping Lord* sequence, with 'the Ram's wife,' probably here a reference to the city of Rome, a counterpart of 'the Lamb's wife', or New Jerusalem, in St John's Apocalypse (Revelation 21:9). A lighthearted reference to some of the many attempts in apocalyptically oriented preaching to find modern historical allegory in every aspect of biblical apocalyptic is afforded by Coleridge, who comments on a 'true lover of liberty' who had 'proved to the satisfaction of many that Mr Pitt was one of the horns of the second beast in The Revelation, that spoke as a dragon' (*Biographia Literaria*, chapter 10).

H. David Brumble
University of Pittsburgh

Leopard Change His Spots

In Jeremiah 13 the prophet is told by the Lord to condemn Judah for its habitual miscreance, castigating with a rhetorical question: 'Can the Ethiopian change his skin, or the leopard his spots? then may ye also do good that are accustomed to do evil' (13:23). In early Christian exegesis these tropes are taken as signifying the natural condition of fallen humanity, 'spotted' with sin in the case of the leopard and naturally without remedy (e.g., St Jerome, *Epistle* 97.2). But still more frequently the figures are used to demonstrate a positive answer to Jeremiah's rhetorical query, asserting that by grace just such radical transformations are possible. With reference to the story of the conversion of the Ethiopian eunuch (Acts 8:27–38) Jerome observes: 'Though it is against nature the Ethiopian does change his skin and the leopard his spots' (*Epistle* 49.6). The Ethiopian eunuch is for him 'a type of the Gentile, who in spite of the prophet changed his skin, and whilst he read the Old Testament found the fountain of the gospel' (*Epistle* 108.11). The force of these allusions is accordingly not, as might at first be imagined, to characterize the incorrigibility of human nature without God, but to demonstrate that what alone can transform it is, as implied in Jeremiah's haranguing interrogation, an obedient response to God.

In medieval manuscript illustrations of the Fall of Adam and Eve a leopard is sometimes placed at their feet, iconographically indicating the state of sinful nature into which they have descended; this motif is replicated in a woodcut on the frontispiece of a 15th-century French Bible. In Chrétien de Troyes' *Erec et Enide*, after Erec has been at last humiliated by Enide into rising from overindulgence in their marriage bed at Carnant, he arms himself for his pilgrimage-quest while standing on a rug which is prominently decorated with a leopard. When in Shakespeare's *Richard III* the King hears Bolingbroke accuse Mowbray of treachery and murder he tries to interpose, saying, 'Give me his gage. Lions make leopards tame.' Mowbray hotly retorts: 'Yea, but not change his spots' (1.1.173–75). Robert Southey offers a similarly prejudicial determination in 'Ode on Negociations with Bonaparte in 1814', warning against unwise diplomacy: 'For sooner shall the Ethiopian change his skin, / Or from the Leopard shall her spots depart, / Than this man change his old flatigious heart.' In Sir Walter Scott's *Talisman*, however, the force of the image to highlight an extraordinary transformation is preserved, when Richard Coeur de Lion praises the 'brave knight of the Leopard', saying, 'thou hast shown that the Ethiopian may change his skin, and the leopard his spots, though clerks quote Scripture for the impossibility.' Scott's reading here implicates the potential for misconstruing Jeremiah's words by overlooking their original subjunctive and optative irony in order to make a merely indicative judgment.

David L. Jeffrey
University of Ottawa

Lion Lies down with the Lamb

One of the characteristics of the messianic kingdom of the future described by Isaiah is a return to prelapsarian innocence, in which 'the wolf also shall dwell with the kid; and the calf and the young lion and the fatling together; and a little child shall lead them... And the lion shall eat straw like the ox' (Isaiah 11:6–7). The passage is frequently rendered as saying 'the lion shall lie down with the lamb'; the text is quoted or alluded to by a number of major English poets, usually in the context of a utopian or millenarian imagination. In Shelley's *Queen Mab* (124–28), for example, the Queen looks forward to such a future, when:

> The lion now forgets to thirst for blood:
> There might you see him sporting in the sun
> Beside the dreadless kid; his claws are sheathed,
> His teeth are harmless, custom's force had made
> His nature as the nature of a lamb.

Henry James, in 'The Death of the Lion', depicts the soirées of socially predatory Mrs Weeks Wimbush, 'proprietress of the universal menagerie', as times in which 'the animals rub shoulders freely with the spectators and the lions sit down for whole evenings with the lambs.' In Margaret Avison's 'Then',

> The leopard and the kid
> are smoothness (fierce)
> and softness (gentle)
> and will lie down together. (*sunblue*, 98)

The phrase 'The lion shall eat straw like the ox' acquires in Blake an antimillenarian response: 'One Law for the Lion & Ox is Oppression'

29

('A Memorable Fancy'; cf. 'Marginalia on Reynold's Discourses'; 'Tiriel', 7.33). The relationship between the 'kingdom of God within' and the messianic millennium is questioned in Anthony Hecht's 'Pig', where also the iconographic association of the lion with St Mark the Evangelist and St Jerome the translator is recalled:

> And all things be redeemed – the suckling babe
> Lie safe in the serpent's home
> And the lion eat straw like the ox and roar its love
> to Mark and to Jerome. (*Hard Hours*, 13)

David L. Jeffrey
University of Ottawa

Man of Sorrows

The 'man of sorrows' of Isaiah 53:5 is identified also (in the so-called 'servant songs' of Isaiah, chapters 42:1–4; 49:1–6; 50:4–9; 52:13 – 53:12) as the 'servant of the Lord'. In exegetical tradition the same figure is commonly referred to as the 'suffering servant'. The character and mission of the servant is described in his own words, in the words of the Lord, and in the words of those to whom he has been sent (the 'we' of Isaiah 53:2–6). The servant has been chosen by God to 'bring forth judgment to the nations' (Isaiah 42:1); he will work patiently, confident that the Lord will in time vindicate the shame and violent scorn which he must endure. The climax of his story comes in the final poem, where those to whom the servant has been sent recognize that this man of sorrows, who is 'despised and rejected' by them (53:3) and apparently judged and afflicted by God, is nevertheless God's instrument to atone for their sins. He is 'wounded for... [their] transgressions' and, despite his own innocence, condemned to die on their behalf. The poem concludes with the reaffirmation that the servant will not suffer in vain and that his mission will succeed.

The identity of the servant has long been the subject of controversy. He has been identified as a historical individual: the prophetic author himself, an anonymous contemporary of the prophet, Moses, Jeremiah, Hezekiah, and Zerubbabel, among others. Early rabbinic commentary was unanimous in seeing the description of the servant as a portrait of the Messiah. (A similar messianic reference occurs in a talmudic legend in which Elijah tells a rabbi seeking the Messiah, 'A man of sorrows himself, he ministers lovingly to those who suffer, and binds up their wounds.') But the concept of a suffering Messiah was generally problematic for later Jewish commentators who, following Rashi in the 11th century, chose rather to see the servant as the embodiment of Israel.

Andrew of St Victor incorporates in his 12th-century commentary on Isaiah Jewish exegetical identification of the suffering servant with the Jews of captivity, or possibly Isaiah himself, not even mentioning a messianic or typological reading (Smalley, 164). For other Christian exegetes, however, the suffering servant was readily identified as Jesus Christ. Christ himself understood his mission in the light of the servant's atonement through suffering and patient endurance, and the early Church reinforced the connection. The description of the Passion and death of Jesus recorded in all four gospels is coloured by references to the 'servant songs' (e.g., Matthew 8:17; Mark 15:28; John 19:9). From the patristic era to the 18th century Christian interpreters were unanimous in seeing the last of the 'servant songs' especially as a prophetic witness to the death of a sinless Christ for the sins of humankind. Martin Luther in his commentary on Isaiah indicates the familiar view of Isaiah 53:3 as a predictive description of Christ's 'physical, open and extremely shameful suffering' (Works, 17.220). Calvin, in his commentary on Isaiah, posits the sorrow and suffering as itself the motivation for humanity's rejection of Christ (4.114). In his sermon of 1 July 1627 John Donne refers to Christ as the type of all sorrow: 'who fulfil'd in himselfe alone, all *Types*, and *Images*, and *Prophecies* of sorrowes, who was, (as the *Prophet* calls him) *Vir dolorum*, a man compos'd, and elemented of sorrowes'. In another sermon (25 August 1622) Donne asks that he himself be allowed to 'be *vir dolorum*, a man of affliction, a vessell baked in that furnace, fitted by God's proportion, and *dosis* of his corrections, to make a right use of his corrections'. In 'Palm Sunday', Henry Vaughan writes of 'the man of sorrow / Weeping still, like the wet morrow', who 'comes to borrow' the 'shades and freshness' of palm branches on his entrance into Jerusalem.

Melville takes quite a different approach when referring to the suffering servant in *Moby Dick*: Ishmael suggests 'that mortal man who hath more of joy than sorrow in him, that mortal man cannot be true – not true, or undeveloped... The truest of all men was the Man of Sorrows.' Yeats' 'The Sad Shepherd' contains echoes of, if not direct references to, the man of sorrows in its description of 'a man whom Sorrow named his friend' and who, because he was not listened to, could not be rid of the 'ancient burden' of his 'heavy story'. Joyce, in *A Portrait of the Artist as a Young Man* (chapter 3), makes more traditional use of the image, as Stephen considers the contrast between the humiliation of the first advent and the glory of the Second Coming.

Other echoes from the 'servant songs' occur in a variety of English texts. Wordsworth, in 'Maternal Grief,' speaks of a small boy whose twin sister has died as suddenly 'acquainted with distress and grief' (Isaiah 53:3). In his 'Stanzas to Augusta [B]' Byron echoes the same passage: 'Thy soul with my grief was acquainted...' Perhaps the most influential use of the man of sorrows motif, however, is Handel's magnificent setting of the final servant song in his *Messiah*.

Marnie Parsons
Wilfrid Laurier University
W. Roger Williams
Marianapolis College, Montreal

Messiah

'Messiah' is a transliteration of Hebrew *mashiah*, an adjective which means 'anointed', and so can refer to anyone with a divinely appointed mission – kings (e.g., 1 Samuel 24:6; Lamentations 4:20), high priests (Leviticus 4:3, 5, 16; 6:22), priests (Exodus 28:41; Leviticus 10:7; Numbers 3:3), and even the Gentile king Cyrus (Isaiah 54:1). The term *mashiah* is not, in fact, ever used in the Old Testament as a reference to Messiah. The King James Version twice mentions 'the Messiah' in the Old Testament, but it is now recognized that 'the anointed one' is a more apt translation, since King James Version's 'the Messiah the Prince' (Daniel 9:25, 'the anointed prince') probably refers to Cyrus (see Isaiah 45:1), and 'the Messiah' (KJV Daniel 9:26, 'anointed one') to Onias III.

The Old Testament does, of course, give voice to messianic longings and expectation. Genesis 49:10 is a very early messianic prophecy: 'The sceptre shall not depart from Judah, nor a lawgiver from between his feet, until Shiloh come; and unto him shall the gathering of the people be.' Moses promised that 'The Lord thy God will raise up unto thee a Prophet... like unto me' (Deuteronomy 18:15). Often such prophecies look forward to a time when Israel would again be united as it had been in the time of David: 'Then shall the children of Judah and the children of Israel be gathered together, and appoint themselves one head' (Hosea 1:11), and at this time 'shall the children of Israel return, and seek the Lord their God, and David their king' (Hosea 3:5; see also Amos 9:11–15). This leader, this new David, will be a scourge to the foes of Israel, such a one as had been prophesied in Numbers 24:17: 'there shall come a Star out of Jacob, and a Sceptre shall rise out of Israel, and shall smite the corners of Moab, and destroy all the children of Sheth.' For the Psalmist this all-powerful, all-conquering king of Israel is 'a priest for ever after the order of Melchizedek' (110:4), a spiritual leader, then, as well as political – and eternal in his rule.

Sometimes this idea of the messianic reunification of Israel is expanded to envision all the peoples of the world coming to Zion. Isaiah gives the most powerful and the most extended expression to such hopes: 'And it shall come to pass in the last days, that the mountain of the Lord's house shall be established in the top of the mountains... and all nations shall flow into it... and they shall beat their swords into plowshares' (Isaiah 2:2–4; Micah 4:1–4); and for a ruler 'there shall come forth a rod out of the stem of Jesse, and a Branch shall grow out of his roots' (Isaiah 11:1–2; Isaiah is recalling the anointing of David, son of Jesse, 1 Samuel 16:1–13). Another image is provided by the 'suffering servant' of Isaiah 40–55, who has 'no beauty that we should desire him' (Isaiah 53:2), one who labours for a time in vain, who suffers at the hands of the wicked, and who dies for his people, a 'Redeemer of Israel' (Isaiah 49:7). Yet this Redeemer will also be 'a light to the Gentiles' and 'salvation unto the end of the earth'. He will 'say to the prisoners, Go forth; to them that are in darkness, Show yourselves' (Isaiah 49:1–9):

> For he shall grow up before him as a tender plant, and as a root out of dry ground... He is despised and rejected of men; a man of sorrows, and acquainted with grief... and we esteemed him not... But he was wounded for our transgressions... and with his stripes we are healed... he is brought as a lamb to the slaughter... his soul an offering for sin. (Isaiah 53:1–10; see also 35:4; 40:10; 42:1–9; 52:13–15; 59:20)

For Daniel the mysterious and awesome figure associated with the triumph of the elect is at once human *and* divine: 'behold, one like the Son of man came with the clouds of heaven, and came to the Ancient of days' (7:13–14).

In the New Testament, where Jewish hopes for a Messiah are seen as fulfilled in Jesus, the evangelists portray Jesus drawing all these – and other – strands together into a single thread of prophecy: 'the Son of man came not to be ministered unto, but to minister, and to give his life up as a ransom for many' (Mark 10:45). In this one passage, Jesus casts himself as 'the Son of man' of Daniel 7:13, as the 'servant' of Isaiah 49:3, and as the suffering Redeemer of Isaiah 53:4–9. Jesus makes explicit his messianic role in John 4:25–26: the Samaritan woman 'saith unto him, I know that Messias cometh, which is called Christ... Jesus saith unto her, I that speak unto thee am he.' And in John 1:41 Andrew says, 'We have found the Messias, which is, being interpreted, the Christ'; indeed, since Christ was the Greek equivalent of Hebrew *mashiah*, 'the anointed one', every reference in the New Testament to Jesus as 'the Christ' is a reference to Jesus as 'the messiah' (see, e.g., Matthew 16:16; Mark 8:29; Luke 2:11; John 10:24; Acts 18:5).

Psalm 110 was given a messianic interpretation at least as early as the time of Jesus, and so was the most widely quoted Psalm in the New Testament: 'Jesus saith unto him... Hereafter shall ye see the Son of man sitting on the right hand of power, and coming in the clouds of heaven' (Matthew 26:64; there is also a reference here to Daniel 7:13; for other New Testament references to Psalm 110, see, e.g., Matthew 22:41–46; Acts 2:34–35; 5:31; 7:55; Romans 8:34; 1 Corinthians 15:25; Ephesians 1:20; Hebrews 1:13; 5:6, 10; 8:1; 10:12–13; Revelation 3:21).

For patristic writers, of course, there was no question that many passages in the Old Testament referred directly to Christ. St Ambrose, for example, writes that Genesis 49:8–12 only 'appears' to refer to Judah, while 'indeed... that later Juda is meant' – Christ (*Fathers of the Church*, 65.251). Ambrose goes on to gloss Isaiah 11:1: 'The root is the household of the Jews, the rod is Mary, the flower of Mary is Christ' (65.252); this interpretation originated with Tertullian, *De carne Christi*, 251.5). St Augustine understands Psalm 1:3 as referring to Christ: 'That "tree" then, that is, our Lord, from "the running streams of water", that is from the sinful people's drawing them by the way into the roots of discipline, will "bring forth fruit", that is, after He hath been glorified' (*Enarrationes in Psalmos*, Nicene and Post-Nicene Fathers, 8.1). The Vulgate sometimes even translates Old Testament 'anointed one' with *Christus* (e.g., Psalm 2:2; Daniel 9:25–26). Indeed, this christological reading of the Old Testament encouraged the Fathers to find references to Christ in a very wide range of Old Testament events; Eve's issuing from a wound in the side of Adam, for example, was seen as a type for the blood issuing from the side of Christ (St John Chrysostom, *Ancient Christian Writers*, 31.62).

The assumption of such passages is that God so arranged the events of history that they would be meaningful, functioning as a broad and detailed prophecy of the Messiah and his mission. History leads up to and is granted retrospective significance in terms of the birth, life, death, and resurrection of Jesus. Subsequent history likewise is adequated to the predicted eschaton: Christian historiography in the Middle Ages is charged with messianic expectation, and numerous attempts were made to correlate proximate historical events to biblical prophecy so as to arrive at a probable date for what Christians anticipated as the Second Coming of Christ. Favoured dates (in their various periods) were AD1000, 1233, 1260, 1300, 1333, 1360, and 1400. But Jewish speculation on the coming of the Messiah and the corresponding millennial reign was comparable: the year 1358 was the favourite Jewish date in the 14th century, though the *De Jure Belli* of Giovanni da Legnano, written in 1360, refers to 1365 as a likely date (ed. T.E. Holland, 1917, 77–78).

The first advent of the Messiah, in a Christian perspective, and expectation of his final coming and judgment, determine the structuring (or restructuring) of biblical narrative in numerous works of medieval English literature. In the 14th century, for example, one typically finds in the cycle plays not only a Prophets' Play, wherein the coming of the Messiah is explicitly foretold, but also such detailed prefigurations as the child-lamb being born to Gil in 'The Second Shepherds' Play'. In book 1 of *The Faerie Queene* one finds not only the messianic structure, with the dragon-devil waiting to be defeated at the coming of the Christ-like Redcrosse Knight, but also such typological details as the child playing with the dragon-serpent (*The Fairie Queen*, 1.12.11) in fulfillment of Isaiah 11:8, 'And the sucking child shall play on the hole of the asp, and the weaned child shall put his hand on the cockatrice's den' (see J.C. Nohrnberg, *The Analogy of the Faerie Queene*).

Eighteenth-century interest in the Eclogues of Virgil and the Sibylline prophecies, thought then to be parallel in many respects to Old Testament prophecies concerning the coming Messiah, encouraged imaginative treatment of some of the chief 'messianic' portions of Isaiah. Alexander Pope freely blends elements from Virgil's *Pollio* eclogue (*Eclogues*, 4, esp. 6–46) and Isaiah (7:14; 11:1; 40:1–4; 45:8, etc.) to create his 'Messiah,' first published in the *Spectator* (1712). Pope's stirring phrases reveal, however, a dominance of scriptural idiom:

> The SAVIOUR comes! by ancient Bards foretold:
> Hear him ye Deaf, and all ye Blind behold!
> He from thick Films shall purge the visual Ray,
> And on the sightless Eye-ball pour the Day.
> 'Tis he th'obstructed Paths of Sound shall clear,
> And bid new Musick charm th'unfolding Ear.
> The Dumb shall sing, the Lame his Crutch foregoe,
> And leap exulting like the bounding Roe. (37–44)

Pope's triumphant concluding lines are consistent with the whole poem in their indebtedness to Isaiah (esp. 51:6; 54:10; 60:19–20):

> One Tyde of Glory, one unclouded Blaze,
> O'erflow thy Courts: The LIGHT HIMSELF shall shine
> Reveal'd; and *God's* eternal Day be thine!

The Seas shall waste; the Skies in Smoke decay;
Rocks fall to Dust, and Mountains melt away;
But fix'd *His* Word, *His* saving Pow'r remains:
Thy Realm for ever lasts! thy own *Messiah* reigns!

The most celebrated *Messiah* of the 18th century is undoubtedly that of G.F. Handel (1742). The oratorio is atypical in Handel's canon in that it tells no story; rather, it sets forth a series of scriptural texts arranged as a litany of meditations on redemption, commencing with a series of Old Testament prophecies (notably centering on Isaiah again) and moving through the ministry of Jesus to the Cross and Resurrection. It was a peculiar accomplishment of Handel's composition that, as William Cowper put it ironically, thousands of auditors with no interest in the Messiah (or, he implies, in redemption) thus heard a fair précis of scriptural salvation history for the sake of Handel's great music. In Cowper's wry reflection:

Man praises man. Desert in arts or arms
Wins public honour; and ten thousand sit
Patiently present at a sacred song,
Commemoration-mad; content to hear
(Oh wonderful effect of music's pow'r!)
Messiah's eulogy for Handel's sake! (*The Task*, 6.632–37)

Cowper's priest, fellow hymn writer (*Olney Hymns*), and mentor at Olney, John Newton, having later become rector at St Mary Woolnoth in London, was happy to take advantage of an extremely successful rerun of Handel's *Messiah* at Westminster Abbey during 1784–85 to preach a remarkable series of fifty sermons. These were published with considerable success as *Messiah: Or, the Scriptural Passages which Form the Subject of the Celebrated Oratorio of Handel* (1786). Handel thus has come to figure largely in English allusions, literary and otherwise, to 'the Messiah'. Interestingly parallel, however, is Friedrich Gottlieb Klopstock's religious epic *Messias*, inspired by Milton's *Paradise Lost*. After appearing in Germany in 1748 and 1773 it became well known also in England and America.

A contrasting deemphasis of the subject, or redefinition of it, becomes apparent in later literature. For Blake, who in *The Marriage of*

Heaven and Hell wants to exalt the Subconscious (or hell) at the expense of Good and Reason, the Messiah becomes simply Desire: 'the Messiah fell, & formed a heaven of what he stole from the abyss' (*Complete Writings*, 1966, 149, pl. 5). In a related vein, Coleridge sees the integrated consciousness or 'whole one Self' as 'the Messiah's destined victory!' ('Religious Musings'). The American poet Robert Lowell, in 'The Quaker Graveyard in Nantucket', asks his readers to see in the killing of a sperm whale a reenactment of the Crucifixion and so calls the whale 'Jonas Messiah' – with a typological pun on Jonah (see also Lowell's 'No Messiah' and 'Once to Every Man and Nation'). Gore Vidal's *Messiah* (1954) is a parodic 'fifth gospel', recounting the life and cult of John Cave, an unlikely saviour and founder of Caveway, a new religion promising solace through death.

The term Messiah or 'new Messiah' occasionally occurs in literature either as a term of derogation or in a purely secularizing sense. Dryden, for example, disparages the motives of the refugee French Huguenots coming to England, suggesting in his Catholic poem *The Hind and the Panther* (1687) that since their motives are really materialist, it is British affluence which is their 'new Messiah by the star' (3.173–78). Similarly, there are references to other 'Christs', such as Oscar Wilde's 'These Christs that die upon the barricades' ('Sonnet to Liberty'). A.M. Klein's acerbic 'Ballad of the Days of the Messiah', from the section 'A Voice was Heard in Ramah', in his *Collected Poems* (1944), bitterly heralds 'Messiah in an armour-metalled tank', the liberation soldier arrived too late to redeem six million Jews. Klein's World War II poetry has many such references to the failure of Messiah to appear in the darkest hours.

H. David Brumble
University of Pittsburgh
David L. Jeffrey
University of Ottawa

Old Men Dream Dreams

'Your old men shall dream dreams, your young men shall see visions' (Joel 2:28) is part of an eschatological prophecy of the outpouring of the Spirit of God at some indefinite future time, and the mention of old men and young men functions as an indication that the spirit of prophecy will extend to all Israel. In his sermon in Acts 2:14–21, St Peter quotes Joel 2:28–32, declaring that the prophecy has been fulfilled in Jesus' sending of the Holy Spirit at Pentecost (2:16–18).

The phrase 'to dream a dream' imitates Hebrew usage; the introduction of this construction into English was influenced by the Vulgate wording of Joel 2:28, *somnia somniabunt* (the usual construction in the Vulgate is *somnium videre*, 'to see a dream'; *somnium somniare* occurs elsewhere only in Jeremiah 29:8). The phrase 'to dream a dream' occurs in English at least as early as the Middle English *Story of Genesis and Exodus* (c. 1250), in a passage where there is no warrant for the redundant construction in the Vulgate text being paraphrased (Early English Text Society, old series 7, 1873, 2095). It occurs frequently throughout the history of English literature, and some writers, such as Shakespeare (*Richard III*, 5.3.212; *Romeo and Juliet*, 1.4.50) and Eugene O'Neill, seem to be particularly fond of it. While not every occurrence of this phrase can be regarded as a conscious allusion to Joel 2:28, there is a variety of English literary allusions which clearly refer to the Joel verse as a whole.

Francis Bacon, in his essay 'Of Youth and Age', refers to a rabbinic opinion which from Joel 2:28 'inferreth that young men are admitted nearer to God than old, because vision is a clearer revelation than a dream' (*Essays*, 1890, 300). Shakespeare possibly alludes to the Joel verse in *Troilus and Cressida* when he has Priam say: 'Come, Hector, come, go back. / Thy wife hath dremt, thy mother hath had visions' (5.3.62–63).

In 'Ivan Ivanovitch' Robert Browning has an ancient Russian priest quote Joel 2:28 as support for the divine authority of his judgment (316–21), and in another Browning poem, 'Mr Sludge, "The Medium"', Sludge pictures his patrons urging him to continue his spiritualism by saying: 'There's no one doubts you, Sludge! / You dream the dreams, you see the spiritual sights' (412–13). Bernard Shaw uses the Joel verse to characterize utopian political thinking in the preface to *Geneva*, and in the preface to *Farfetched Fables* he concludes a list of great thinkers and artists of the past with this: 'to say nothing of living seers of visions and dreamers of dreams'. In *Man and Superman* Shaw has John Tanner say that a true artist knows that women 'have the power to rouse his deepest creative energies, to rescue him from his cold reason, to make him see visions and dream dreams' (*Works*, 1930, 10.24). In his 'Laments for a Dying Language 3', Ogden Nash satirizes bureaucratic euphemisms:

> To the sociologist squeamish
> The words 'Your old men shall dream dreams'
>   are less than beamish,
> so 'Your senior citizens shall dream dreams'
>   it shall henceforth be,
> Along with Hemingway's 'The Senior Citizen and the Sea'.
> (*I Wouldn't Have Missed It*, 1975, 330.8–11)

Lawrence T. Martin
University of Akron

Peace, When There is no Peace

This saying, part of Jeremiah's denunciation of the total corruption of the people of Judah (Jeremiah 6:14; 8:11), is echoed in a similar context in Ezekiel 13:10. 'Peace, peace' is the superficial response of priest and prophet (also scribe and wise man, Jeremiah 8:8–9) to the incurable 'hurt of the daughter of my people'. J. Bright (*Jeremiah*, Anchor Bible 45) captures the sense well: 'They treat my people's fracture with nostrums, and cry "It is well! It is well!" but it is not well!' Ezekiel adds the image of daubing a loosely constructed wall with whitewash (KJV 'untempered mortar' is inaccurate), as if that would protect it against storms.

False prophets who said what people wanted to hear and earned their living by so doing are frequently attacked in the Old Testament (e.g., Jeremiah 23:16–22; Micah 3:5). 'Thus they degrade themselves into pledged supporters of every piece of wishful thinking' (W. Eichrodt, *Ezekiel*, 1970, 168). In Jeremiah's day there was a rooted conviction that God was pledged to protect his people, come what may, and the false prophets played on this.

'Peace' in these passages, as always in the Old Testament, does not signify merely absence of war, but total well-being. Henry Vaughan is concerned with the spiritual state of the believer's heart when in 'The Check' he bemoans the lack of inner or outer peace; in 'Affliction' he speaks of how, in the practical life of a follower of Christ, it may be that 'Peace, peace; it is not so'. The passage from Jeremiah is nevertheless often invoked in time of war, or a threat of war. Two such instances of renown are themselves the source of many subsequent allusions. One of Patrick Henry's most famous speeches (1775) includes the lines: 'Gentlemen cry peace, peace, when there is no peace. I know not what course others may take; but as for me, give me liberty, or give me death!' Neville Chamberlain's ill-fated words of a century and a half later are recalled in their biblical (and liturgical) context, 'Give us peace in our time, O Lord', by David Jones in his *Anathemata* (7.186).

R.T. France
Wycliffe Hall, Oxford, England

Seraph

Seraphim (singular, *seraph*), from Hebrew *saraph* ('fiery'), appear in the Bible only in Isaiah 6:1–7, where they are described as six-winged creatures standing above God's throne and repeating in loud voices the chant which has become known in Christian tradition as the 'trisagion': 'Holy, holy, holy, is the Lord of hosts: the whole earth is full of his glory' (v. 3; cf. the *Te Deum* canticle of Morning Prayer in the Book of Common Prayer, lines 3–5). Seraphim are not primarily 'messengers' (angels) but are rather attendants on God and celebrants of his holiness and power. In Revelation 4:8, the four beasts of the Apocalypse have six wings and recite the trisagion, representing an apparent conflation of the creatures of Isaiah 6 with those of Ezekiel 1:5–14.

In Jewish lore seraphim function as angels: they are messengers between God and man in Paradise, perform the last rites on Adam, and intimidate evil spirits so that they fear to do harm to humankind. They are especially remarkable for their wings (often allegorized), their loud voices (lightning flashes and fiery darts issue from their mouths), and their prodigious size (it would take 500 years to traverse their length and breadth). The prince of the seraphim is variously given as Seraphiel, Metatron, Michael, Jaoel, and Satan (before his fall).

Early Christian exegetes, notably Pseudo-Dionysius (*De caelesti hierarchia*, 7), made the seraphim the highest of nine orders of angels

– an eminence not seriously challenged in Christian angelology until the 16th century – and medieval poets followed patristic example (e.g., Dante, *Paradiso*, 27.98–126). The Protestant Reformers, however, regarded the Dionysian system as overly elaborate and a pious fraud: 'If we would be duly wise,' Calvin counsels (*Institutes*, 1.14.4), 'we must renounce those vain babblings of idle men, concerning the nature, ranks, and number of angels.'

In Christian art, seraphim are usually red (denoting fire) and carry a *flabellum* (flaming sword) with the inscription 'Holy, holy, holy'.

Postmedieval references in English, given Protestant antipathy to the Dionysian system, tend to be brief, few in number, and rigidly scriptural in imagery: for example, Spenser's 'eternal burning *Seraphins*' ('An Hymne of Heavenly Beauty', 94) and Vaughan's 'flaming ministrie' ('The Search', 60). An exception is Crashaw's baroque preconversion poem on St Teresa, the full title of which is 'The Flaming Heart vpon the Book and Picture of the seraphicall saint TERESA, (as she is vsvally expressed with a Seraphim biside her)'. Milton, on the other hand, represents a more typical English attitude: the term *seraph* is used in *Paradise Lost* as a periphrasis for *angel* (e.g., 1.794; 7.198), and the prominent angels in the poem (Satan, Raphael, Michael) are archangels, not seraphim, although Raphael is once called a seraph and described as having six wings (5.277–85). There is an interesting invocation of Isaiah 6:6–7 in the autobiographical Preface to book 2 of *Reason of Church Government* (1642), where Milton links his poetic vocation with the Old Testament prophets' calling and asserts that God 'sends out his Seraphim with the hallow'd fire of his Altar to touch and purify the lips of whom he pleases' (*Prose Works*, Yale ed., 1.821).

Apart from Pope (*Essay on Man*, 1.110, 278; *Eloisa to Abelard*, 218, 320), few references appear in 18th-century literature. With the Romantics and Victorians, however, there is a resurgence of interest. Blake adopts seraphim as the spirits of love, whose symbol is fire (e.g., *Jerusalem*, 86.24–25) and makes Mne Seraphim (a version of *Bne Seraphim* = 'the sons of the Seraphim') the parent of Thel and her sisters (*Thel*, 1.1). In *The Rime of the Ancient Mariner* Coleridge draws on the medieval symbology of seraphim as angels of love and light when the shining 'seraph-band' enspirits the mariner's shipmates and brings the stricken ship to safe harbour (488–95). There is an allusion to 'burning seraphs' in Wordsworth (*Prelude*, 10.522), and the traditional associations of Christian exegesis – seraphim as messengers of fire and love – are rehearsed in Byron's *Cain* (1.133, 418) and in Elizabeth Barrett Browning's 1051-line dramatic lyric 'The Seraphim' (1838), which imagines the Crucifixion as seen through the eyes of two sentimental seraphim named Ador and Zerah. Byron (*Don Juan*, 3.258; 4.881) together with Keats (*Eve of St Agnes*, 275–76) led the way in the secularization of seraph as a synonym either for 'angelic' intellect (Tennyson, *Palace of Art*, 133; *In Memoriam*, 30.27; 109.5) or, more commonly, 'angelic' female beauty (Browning, *The Ring and the Book*, 6.1492). In Dickens' 'Mrs Lirriper's Lodgings' (*Christmas Stories*, 1871), Seraphina, the heroine, is described as 'the most beautiful creature that ever was seen, and she had brown eyes, and she had brown hair all curling beautifully, and she had a delicious voice, and she was delicious altogether.' This creature, like Shaw's languid temptress Seraphita Lunn in *Overruled* (1912), is a long way from the winged guardians of God's throne in Isaiah's vision.

More interesting – and arresting – treatments, however, do occur. In Twain's *Huckleberry Finn* (chapter 17), Emmeline Grangerford's 'greatest picture,' unfinished at her death, depicts 'a young woman in a long white gown... [who] had two arms folded across her breast, and two arms stretched out in front, and two more reaching up towards the moon – and the idea was, to see which pair would look best and then scratch out all the other arms.'

In Rudy Wiebe's wry tale 'The Angel of the Tar Sands', Alberta oil workers dig up a seraph who flexes its wings ('three sets of wings now sweeping back and forth as if loosening up in some seraphic 5BX plan') and roars at them in low German before flying off (*The Angel of the Tar Sands and Other Stories*, 1982).

John Spencer Hill
University of Ottawa

Swords into Ploughshares

'They shall beat their swords into plowshares', a generally recognized image for the cessation of war, occurs in Isaiah 2:4 and Micah 4:3 in similar descriptions of the universal peace of the messianic age, when Jerusalem is to be the spiritual centre of the world and God the arbiter of disputes and judge of nations. The image is reversed in Joel 3:10 in an ironic challenge from God to the Gentile 'men of war', as he calls those nations to judgment in 'the valley of decision': 'Beat your plowshares into swords and your pruning hooks into spears.'

The sword is the usual Old Testament *hereb*, usually a short, straight, two-edged blade for close fighting, generally associated in the Old Testament and New Testament with violence, oppression, and God's vengeance. The plowshare (Hebrew *'et*, also meaning 'hoe', 'mattock', or a 'digging tool' in general) is simply the digging end of the primitive plow, the sharpened end of the handle-stick; by David's time most shares were sheathed in iron.

Swords and plowshares may well have been commonplace symbols of war and peace in the ancient world. In Virgil's *Georgics*, written specifically to promote the peaceful arts of agriculture after the ravages of civil war, imagery similar to that of Joel 3:10 is used to describe war prevailing over peace – *et curvae rigidem falces conflatur in ensem* – 'And straight spears were forged from the curved sickle.'

For some patristic and medieval commentators the conversion of swords to plowshares symbolizes a moral transformation by which fierce minds are changed to good and productive ones (Tertullian, Ante-Nicene Fathers 3.346). Lapide provides an extensive commentary on this image as representing the new reign of Christ in the individual Christian: the bodily members and senses which were weapons of the devil are turned into plowshares tilling God's field of works of charity; however, the inner battle of fleshly desires against those of the Spirit continues; he cites Hugh of St Victor's application of Joel 3:10 – the 'plowshares' of mortified bodily members are converted to spiritual weapons to guard faith (*Commentary* 11.124; 13.521; see also St Athanasius, *De incarnatione verbi Dei*, 52).

Plowing is also connected with the Word of God (Isaiah 2:3; Micah 4:2), imaged throughout the Old Testament and New Testament as a 'two-edged sword'; patristic commentators give the plowshare to Christ, in whose hands it penetrates the soul much as does the sword of the Word in Hebrews 4:12. Thus St Jerome in his commentary on Isaiah 2:4 argues that 'when all the hardness of our hearts has been broken by Christ's plow, and the thorny weeds of our vices have been eradicated, then the seeds of God's word can grow up in the furrows.' Similarly, St Bonaventure's discussion of the 'plowshares' of the word of God, referring to the preaching of gospel truth (*Opera Omnia*, 9.565), draws on the New Testament use of plowing as an image for the apostolic mission (Luke 9:62; 1 Corinthians 9:10).

References to swords and plowshares follow three main strands in English literary usage: (1) the New Testament and patristic concept of the preacher / apostle as plowman, (2) the straightforward image of a time of peace and its ironic reversal, and (3) the apocalyptic plowing under of the old creation so that the new can spring forth. *Piers Plowman* is most significant in establishing the tradition of the plowman as both visionary and righteous preacher, drawing from traditional symbolism which suggests that plowing prepares the heart to receive the word of truth and that the plowshare is the tongue (or word) of the preacher (see S. Barney, 276–77). Plowing also symbolizes the true priestly functions of preaching and praying: in the satire on clerical worldliness in Passus 15 of *Piers Plowman* the priest must replace his gilt-edged sword with the 'plow' of the breviary (120–23). In the 18th century, Cowper echoes the idea of the plowshare of Scripture in 'Truth', 459–62:

> But the same word that, like the polished share,
> Ploughs up the roots of a believer's care,
> Kills the flowery weeds, where'er they grow,
> That bind the sinner's Bacchanalian brow.

And in the mid-19th century Browning's villainous Guido (*The Ring and the Book*, 11.1505–10), after vilifying the lust and greed of the clergy, draws ironically on the traditional spiritual interpretation of converting 'members' to righteousness, which evidently formed part of church teaching and counselling:

> I, boast such passions? 'Twas, 'Suppress them straight!
> Or stay, we'll pick and choose before destroy:
> Here's wrath in you, – a serviceable sword, –
> Beat it into a ploughshare! What's this long
> Lance-like ambition? Forge a pruning-hook,
> May be of service when our vines grow tall!'

Allusions to the swords / plowshares prophecies appear most frequently in the traditional war and peace context. Langland quotes Isaiah 2:4 directly when describing the millennial reign of God's justice (*Piers Plowman*, B.3.295–326), adding to it an element of the judgment of Matthew 26:52: all who bear weapons will be condemned to death unless they forge them into sickles and scythes. The image became popular in the Romantic period as part of the vision of the new age which the power of imagination can help bring into being. It is used in Shelley's 'The Witch of Atlas', where the witch writes dreams of the age to come on the brains of the dead who sleep and soldiers dream 'that they [are] blacksmiths... Beating their swords to plowshares'. Hardy uses the traditional interpretation of Isaiah 2:4 to drive home the point that 'the Christian era is *not* one of peace' ('Leipzig, 1813'):

> 'O', the old folks said, 'ye Preachers stern!'
> O so-called Christian time!
> When will men's swords to ploughshares turn?
> When come the promised prime?

In his well-known 'In Time of "The Breaking of Nations"', however, Hardy draws on the allusion more indirectly, using the associations of plowing, a seemingly insignificant yet timeless activity, to make war seem ephemeral.

Allusions to Joel 3:10, where agricultural tools become weapons, are sprinkled throughout the literary canon; one notable instance is in Sidney's *Old Arcadia*, describing the riot in which the mob converts 'husbandry to soldiery', making 'things serviceable for the lives of men, to be the instruments of their deaths'. Occasionally the images of sword and plowshare are conflated. In Marlowe's *Dido, Queen of Carthage*, Dido calls upon her descendant (Alexander) to avenge her on Aeneas by 'ploughing up his countries with his sword' (5.1.308), and in Blake's version of the Samson story Manoa cries that 'our country is plowed with swords, and reaped in blood!' D.H. Lawrence, in *The Man Who Died*, draws on the Old Testament plow of devastation to underline the cyclical nature of earthly life, destroying as it goes:

Let the earth remain earthy... The ploughshare of devastation will be set in the soil of Judea, and the life of this peasant will be overturned like the sods of the field. No man can save the earth from tillage. It is tillage, not salvation.

In Christian eschatology, the destructive nature of plowing ultimately redeems the natural creation, as in Francis Thompson's 'Song of the Hours':

Through earth, sea, and Heaven a doom shall be driven,
    And, sown in the furrows it plougheth,
As fire bursts from stubble,
    Shall spring the new wonders none troweth.

Blake is a significant later exponent of the swords and plowshares image: it runs throughout his writings in various applications, and the 'Plow of Ages' and 'starry harvest' of creation are dominant images of his apocalyptic vision. In a passage which appears both in *Four Zoas* ('Night the Seventh', 170–79) and *Jerusalem* (chapter 3, pl. 65), Blake uses the imagery of Joel 3:10 to embody his contention that materialistic reasoning and delight in machinery for its own sake lead inevitably to violence: the 'sons of Urizen' (associated with the reasoning power in humans) leave 'the plow & harrow' to forge the sword, chariot, and battle axe – 'And all the arts of life they changed to arts of death.' The sons contemn the hourglass and waterwheel as the simple workmanship of 'the plowman' and 'the shepherd'. The end of earthly time, however, sees Urizen at his true work, tilling 'the wide universal field' of the creation with 'the Plow of Ages' and sowing 'the seed' of human souls to await the final Resurrection (*Four Zoas*, 'Night the Ninth', 335–38). In *Milton* that apocalyptic plowing causes the tribulations of the end time; but the violent role of the plow in that time is most vividly portrayed in the climactic scene in *Jerusalem* (chapter 3, pl. 56), where Albion (Mankind) falls under his plow. Having become subservient to his rational nature,... 'Albion fled from the Divine Vision; with the Plow of Nations enflaming, / The Living Creatures madden'd, and Albion fell into the Furrow; and / the Plow went over him & the Living was Plowed in among the Dead.' In Blake's eschatology, this plowing under of both the quick and the dead precedes the final Resurrection, a parallel further supported by Jesus' death and subsequent resurrection in 35–36: 'Who fell beneath his instruments of husbandry & became Subservient to the clods of the furrow...'

Katherine Quinsey
University of Windsor

PROPHETS BEFORE THE EXILE

Amos

Hosea

First Isaiah

Micah

Zephaniah

Nahum

Habakkuk

Jeremiah

Amos

GOD'S JUDGMENTS ON THE NATIONS
Amos 1:1–2, 9 – 2:16

The words of Amos, who was among the herdmen of Tekoa, which he saw concerning Israel in the days of Uzziah king of Judah, and in the days of Jeroboam the son of Joash king of Israel, two years before the earthquake. And he said,

> The Lord will roar from Zion,
>> and utter his voice from Jerusalem;
> and the habitations of the shepherds shall mourn,
>> and the top of Carmel shall wither...

Thus saith the Lord;

> For three transgressions of Tyrus,
>> and for four, I will not turn away the punishment thereof;
> because they delivered up the whole captivity to Edom,
>> and remembered not the brotherly covenant:
> But I will send a fire on the wall of Tyrus,
>> which shall devour the palaces thereof.

Thus saith the Lord;

> For three transgressions of Edom,
>> and for four, I will not turn away the punishment thereof;
> because he did pursue his brother with the sword,
>> and did cast off all pity, and his anger did tear perpetually,
>> and he kept his wrath for ever:
> But I will send a fire upon Teman,
>> which shall devour the palaces of Bozrah.

Thus saith the Lord;

> For three transgressions of the children of Ammon,
>> and for four, I will not turn away the punishment thereof;

because they have ripped up the women with child of Gilead,
    that they might enlarge their border:
But I will kindle a fire in the wall of Rabbah,
    and it shall devour the palaces thereof,
with shouting in the day of battle,
    with a tempest in the day of the whirlwind:
And their king shall go into captivity,
    he and his princes together,
        saith the Lord.

Thus saith the Lord;

For three transgressions of Moab,
    and for four, I will not turn away the punishment thereof;
because he burned the bones
    of the king of Edom into lime:
But I will send a fire upon Moab,
    and it shall devour the palaces of Kirioth:
and Moab shall die with tumult, with shouting,
    and with the sound of the trumpet:
And I will cut off the judge from the midst thereof,
    and will slay all the princes thereof with him,
        saith the Lord.

Thus saith the Lord;

For three transgressions of Judah,
    and for four, I will not turn away the punishment thereof;
because they have despised the law of the Lord,
    and have not kept his commandments,
and their lies caused them to err,
    after the which their fathers have walked:
But I will send a fire upon Judah,
    and it shall devour the palaces of Jerusalem.

Thus saith the Lord;

For three transgressions of Israel,
    and for four, I will not turn away the punishment thereof;

because they sold the righteous for silver,
    and the poor for a pair of shoes;
That pant after the dust of the earth on the head of the poor,
    and turn aside the way of the meek:
and a man and his father will go in unto the same maid,
    to profane my holy name:
And they lay themselves down
    upon clothes laid to pledge by every altar,
and they drink the wine of the condemned
    in the house of their god.

Yet destroyed I the Amorite before them,
    whose height was like the height of the cedars,
    and he was strong as the oaks;
yet I destroyed his fruit from above,
    and his roots from beneath.

Also I brought you up from the land of Egypt,
    and led you forty years through the wilderness,
    to possess the land of the Amorite.
And I raised up of your sons for prophets,
    and of your young men for Nazarites.
Is it not even thus, O ye children of Israel?
        saith the Lord.

But ye gave the Nazarites wine to drink;
    and commanded the prophets, saying, Prophesy not.

Behold, I am pressed under you,
    as a cart is pressed that is full of sheaves.
Therefore the flight shall perish from the swift,
    and the strong shall not strengthen his force,
    neither shall the mighty deliver himself:
Neither shall he stand that handleth the bow;
    and he that is swift of foot shall not deliver himself:
    neither shall he that rideth the horse deliver himself.
And he that is courageous among the mighty
    shall flee away naked in that day,
        saith the Lord.

THE POWER OF PROPHECY
Amos 3:1–8

Hear this word that the Lord hath spoken against you, O children of Israel, against the whole family which I brought up from the land of Egypt, saying,

You only have I known of all the families of the earth:
therefore I will punish you for all your iniquities.

Can two walk together,
except they be agreed?
Will a lion roar in the forest,
when he hath no prey?
will a young lion cry out of his den,
if he have taken nothing?
Can a bird fall in a snare upon the earth,
where no gin is for him?
shall one take up a snare from the earth,
and have taken nothing at all?
Shall a trumpet be blown in the city,
and the people not be afraid?
shall there be evil in a city,
and the Lord hath not done it?

Surely the Lord God will do nothing,
but he revealeth his secret unto his servants the prophets.

The lion hath roared, who will not fear?
the Lord God hath spoken, who can but prophesy?

GOD APPEALS TO HIS PEOPLE
Amos 5:1–4, 8, 11–17

Hear ye this word which I take up against you, even a lamentation, O house of Israel.

The virgin of Israel is fallen;
she shall no more rise:

she is forsaken upon her land;
  there is none to raise her up.

For thus saith the Lord God;

  The city that went out by a thousand
    shall leave an hundred,
  and that which went forth by an hundred
    shall leave ten, to the house of Israel.

For thus saith the Lord unto the house of Israel,

  Seek ye me, and ye shall live...
  Seek him that maketh the seven stars and Orion,
    and turneth the shadow of death into the morning,
    and maketh the day dark with night:
  that calleth for the waters of the sea,
    and poureth them out upon the face of the earth:
  The Lord is his name...

  Forasmuch therefore as your treading is upon the poor,
    and ye take from him burdens of wheat:
  ye have built houses of hewn stone,
    but ye shall not dwell in them;
  ye have planted pleasant vineyards,
    but ye shall not drink wine of them.
  For I know your manifold transgressions
    and your mighty sins:
  they afflict the just, they take a bribe,
    and they turn aside the poor in the gate from their right.
  Therefore the prudent shall keep silence in that time;
    for it is an evil time.

  Seek good, and not evil,
    that ye may live:
  and so the Lord, the God of hosts,
    shall be with you,
    as ye have spoken.
  Hate the evil, and love the good,
    and establish judgment in the gate:

it may be that the Lord God of hosts will be gracious
  unto the remnant of Joseph.

Therefore the Lord, the God of hosts, the Lord, saith thus;

Wailing shall be in all streets;
  and they shall say in all the highways, Alas! alas!
and they shall call the husbandman to mourning,
  and such as are skilful of lamentation to wailing.
And in all vineyards shall be wailing:
  for I will pass through thee,
    saith the Lord.

THE DAY OF THE LORD
Amos 5:18–27

Woe unto you that desire the day of the Lord!
  to what end is it for you?
the day of the Lord is darkness,
  and not light.
As if a man did flee from a lion,
  and a bear met him;
or went into the house, and leaned his hand on the wall,
  and a serpent bit him.
Shall not the day of the Lord be darkness, and not light?
  even very dark, and no brightness in it?
I hate, I despise your feast days,
  and I will not smell in your solemn assemblies.
Though ye offer me burnt offerings and your meat offerings,
  I will not accept them:
neither will I regard the peace offerings of your fat beasts.
Take thou away from me the noise of thy songs;
  for I will not hear the melody of thy viols.
But let judgment run down as waters,
  and righteousness as a mighty stream.

Have ye offered unto me sacrifices
  and offerings

in the wilderness forty years,
  O house of Israel?
But ye have borne the tabernacle of your Moloch and Chiun
  your images, the star of your god,
  which ye made to yourselves.
Therefore will I cause you to go into captivity
  beyond Damascus,
      saith the Lord, whose name is The God of hosts.

FALSE SECURITY
Amos 6:1–7

Woe to them that are at ease in Zion,
  and trust in the mountain of Samaria,
which are named chief of the nations,
  to whom the house of Israel came!
Pass ye unto Calneh, and see;
  and from thence go ye to Hamath the great:
then go down to Gath of the Philistines:
  be they better than these kingdoms?
  or their border greater than your border?
Ye that put far away the evil day,
  and cause the seat of violence to come near;
That lie upon beds of ivory,
  and stretch themselves upon their couches,
  and eat the lambs out of the flock,
  and the calves out of the midst of the stall;
That chant to the sound of the viol,
  and invent to themselves instruments of musick, like David;
That drink wine in bowls,
  and anoint themselves with the chief ointments:
  but they are not grieved for the affliction of Joseph.
Therefore now shall they go captive
  with the first that go captive,
and the banquet of them that stretched themselves
  shall be removed.

THE PLUMBLINE
Amos 7:7–9

Thus he shewed me: and, behold, the Lord stood upon a wall made by a plumbline, with a plumbline in his hand. And the Lord said unto me, Amos, what seest thou? And I said, A plumbline.

Then said the Lord, Behold, I will set a plumbline in the midst of my people Israel: I will not again pass by them any more:

And the high places of Isaac shall be desolate,
and the sanctuaries of Israel shall be laid waste;
and I will rise against the house of Jeroboam with the sword.

THE PRIEST AND THE PROPHET
Amos 7:10–17

Then Amaziah the priest of Bethel sent to Jeroboam king of Israel, saying, Amos hath conspired against thee in the midst of the house of Israel: the land is not able to bear all his words. For thus Amos saith,

Jeroboam shall die by the sword,
and Israel shall surely be led away captive
out of their own land.

Also Amaziah said unto Amos, O thou seer, go, flee thee away into the land of Judah, and there eat bread, and prophesy there: but prophesy not again any more at Bethel: for it is the king's chapel, and it is the king's court.

Then answered Amos, and said to Amaziah, I was no prophet, neither was I a prophet's son; but I was an herdman, and a gatherer of sycomore fruit: and the Lord took me as I followed the flock, and the Lord said unto me, Go, prophesy unto my people Israel. Now therefore hear thou the word of the Lord: thou sayest,

Prophesy not against Israel,
and drop not thy word against the house of Isaac.

Therefore thus saith the Lord;

Thy wife shall be an harlot in the city,
and thy sons and thy daughters shall fall by the sword,
and thy land shall be divided by line;
and thou shalt die in a polluted land:
and Israel shall surely go into captivity forth of his land.

THE BASKET OF FRUIT
Amos 8:1–3

Thus hath the Lord God shewed unto me: and behold a basket of summer fruit. And he said, Amos, what seest thou? And I said, A basket of summer fruit.

Then said the Lord unto me, The end is come upon my people of Israel; I will not again pass by them any more. And the songs of the temple shall be howlings in that day, saith the Lord God: there shall be many dead bodies in every place; they shall cast them forth with silence.

AGAINST INJUSTICE AND OPPRESSION
Amos 8:4–10

Hear this, O ye that swallow up the needy,
even to make the poor of the land to fail,
Saying,
When will the new moon be gone,
that we may sell corn?
and the sabbath,
that we may set forth wheat,
making the ephah small, and the shekel great,
and falsifying the balances by deceit?
That we may buy the poor for silver,
and the needy for a pair of shoes;
yea, and sell the refuse of the wheat?

The Lord hath sworn by the excellency of Jacob, Surely I will never forget any of their works.

> Shall not the land tremble for this,
>> and every one mourn that dwelleth therein?
> and it shall rise up wholly as a flood;
>> and it shall be cast out and drowned,
>> as by the flood of Egypt.

And it shall come to pass in that day, saith the Lord God, that I will cause the sun to go down at noon, and I will darken the earth in the clear day:

> And I will turn your feasts into mourning,
>> and all your songs into lamentation;
> and I will bring up sackcloth upon all loins,
>> and baldness upon every head;
> and I will make it as the mourning of an only son,
>> and the end thereof as a bitter day.

A PROMISE OF RESTORATION
Amos 9:11-15

> In that day will I raise up the tabernacle of David that is fallen,
>> and close up the breaches thereof;
> and I will raise up his ruins,
>> and I will build it as in the days of old:
> That they may possess the remnant of Edom,
>> and of all the heathen, which are called by my name,
>>> saith the Lord that doeth this.

> Behold, the days come,
>>> saith the Lord,
> that the plowman shall overtake the reaper,
>> and the treader of grapes him that soweth seed;
> and the mountains shall drop sweet wine,
>> and all the hills shall melt.

And I will bring again the captivity of my people of Israel,
   and they shall build the waste cities, and inhabit them;
and they shall plant vineyards, and drink the wine thereof;
   they shall also make gardens, and eat the fruit of them.
And I will plant them upon their land,
   and they shall no more be pulled up out of their land
   which I have given them,
      saith the Lord thy God.

Hosea

HOSEA'S WIFE AND CHILDREN
Hosea 1:1 – 2:23

The word of the Lord that came unto Hosea, the son of Beeri, in the days of Uzziah, Jotham, Ahaz, and Hezekiah, kings of Judah, and in the days of Jeroboam the son of Joash, king of Israel.

The beginning of the word of the Lord by Hosea. And the Lord said to Hosea, Go, take unto thee a wife of whoredoms and children of whoredoms: for the land hath committed great whoredom, departing from the Lord. So he went and took Gomer the daughter of Diblaim; which conceived, and bare him a son.

And the Lord said unto him, Call his name Jezreel; for yet a little while, and I will avenge the blood of Jezreel upon the house of Jehu, and will cause to cease the kingdom of the house of Israel. And it shall come to pass at that day, that I will break the bow of Israel, in the valley of Jezreel.

And she conceived again, and bare a daughter. And God said unto him, Call her name Loruhamah: for I will no more have mercy upon the house of Israel; but I will utterly take them away. But I will have mercy upon the house of Judah, and will save them by the Lord their God, and will not save them by bow, nor by sword, nor by battle, by horses, nor by horsemen.

Now when she had weaned Loruhamah, she conceived, and bare a son. Then said God, Call his name Loammi: for ye are not my people, and I will not be your God.

Yet the number of the children of Israel shall be as the sand of the sea, which cannot be measured nor numbered; and it shall come to pass, that in the place where it was said unto them, Ye are not my people, there it shall be said unto them, Ye are the sons of the living God. Then shall the children of Judah and the children of Israel be gathered together, and appoint themselves one head, and they shall come up out of the land: for great shall be the day of Jezreel.

Say ye unto your brethren, Ammi; and to your sisters, Ruhamah.

Plead with your mother, plead:
> for she is not my wife,
> neither am I her husband:

let her therefore put away her whoredoms out of her sight,
> and her adulteries from between her breasts;

Lest I strip her naked,
> and set her as in the day that she was born,

and make her as a wilderness,
> and set her like a dry land, and slay her with thirst.

And I will not have mercy upon her children;
> for they be the children of whoredoms.

For their mother hath played the harlot:
> she that conceived them hath done shamefully:

for she said, I will go after my lovers,
> that give me my bread and my water, my wool and my flax,
> mine oil and my drink.

Therefore, behold, I will hedge up thy way with thorns,
> and make a wall, that she shall not find her paths.

And she shall follow after her lovers,
> but she shall not overtake them;

and she shall seek them,
> but shall not find them:

then shall she say, I will go and return to my first husband;
> for then was it better with me than now.

For she did not know that I gave her corn,
> and wine, and oil,

and multiplied her silver and gold,
> which they prepared for Baal.

Therefore will I return,
> and take away my corn in the time thereof,
> and my wine in the season thereof,

and will recover my wool and my flax
> given to cover her nakedness.

And now will I discover her lewdness in the sight of her lovers,
> and none shall deliver her out of mine hand.

I will also cause all her mirth to cease, her feast days,
 her new moons, and her sabbaths, and all her solemn feasts.
And I will destroy her vines and her fig trees,
 whereof she hath said,
 These are my rewards that my lovers have given me:
and I will make them a forest,
 and the beasts of the field shall eat them.
And I will visit upon her the days of Baalim,
 wherein she burned incense to them,
and she decked herself with her earrings and her jewels,
 and she went after her lovers, and forgat me,
  saith the Lord.

Therefore, behold, I will allure her,
 and bring her into the wilderness,
 and speak comfortably unto her.
And I will give her her vineyards from thence,
 and the valley of Achor for a door of hope:
and she shall sing there, as in the days of her youth,
 and as in the day when she came up out of the land of Egypt.

And it shall be at that day, saith the Lord,
 that thou shalt call me Ishi; and shalt call me no more Baali.
For I will take away the names of Baalim out of her mouth,
 and they shall no more be remembered by their name.
And in that day will I make a covenant for them
 with the beasts of the field and with the fowls of heaven,
 and with the creeping things of the ground:
and I will break the bow and the sword
 and the battle out of the earth,
 and will make them to lie down safely.
And I will betroth thee unto me for ever;
 yea, I will betroth thee unto me in righteousness,
 and in judgment, and in lovingkindness, and in mercies.
I will even betroth thee unto me in faithfulness:
 and thou shalt know the Lord.

And it shall come to pass in that day, I will hear,
  saith the Lord,

I will hear the heavens, and they shall hear the earth;
And the earth shall hear the corn, and the wine, and the oil;
   and they shall hear Jezreel.
And I will sow her unto me in the earth;
   and I will have mercy upon her that had not obtained mercy;
and I will say to them which were not my people,
   Thou art my people;
and they shall say,
   Thou art my God.

HOSEA'S LOVE FOR HIS UNFAITHFUL WIFE
Hosea 3

Then said the Lord unto me, Go yet, love a woman beloved of her friend, yet an adulteress, according to the love of the Lord toward the children of Israel, who look to other gods, and love flagons of wine.

So I bought her to me for fifteen pieces of silver, and for an homer of barley, and an half homer of barley: and I said unto her, Thou shalt abide for me many days; thou shalt not play the harlot, and thou shalt not be for another man: so will I also be for thee.

For the children of Israel shall abide many days without a king, and without a prince, and without a sacrifice, and without an image, and without an ephod, and without teraphim: afterward shall the children of Israel return, and seek the Lord their God, and David their king; and shall fear the Lord and his goodness in the latter days.

GOD'S JUDGMENT ON ISRAEL
Hosea 4:1–10, 6:1–7, 8:1–7

Hear the word of the Lord,
   ye children of Israel:
for the Lord hath a controversy
   with the inhabitants of the land,
because there is no truth, nor mercy,
   nor knowledge of God in the land.

By swearing, and lying, and killing,
   and stealing, and committing adultery,
     they break out, and blood toucheth blood.
Therefore shall the land mourn,
   and every one that dwelleth therein shall languish,
with the beasts of the field, and with the fowls of heaven;
   yea, the fishes of the sea also shall be taken away.

Yet let no man strive, nor reprove another:
   for thy people are as they that strive with the priest.
Therefore shalt thou fall in the day,
   and the prophet also shall fall with thee in the night,
   and I will destroy thy mother.
My people are destroyed for lack of knowledge:
   because thou hast rejected knowledge,
I will also reject thee,
   that thou shalt be no priest to me:
seeing thou hast forgotten the law of thy God,
   I will also forget thy children.
As they were increased, so they sinned against me:
   therefore will I change their glory into shame.
They eat up the sin of my people,
   and they set their heart on their iniquity.
And there shall be, like people, like priest:
   and I will punish them for their ways,
   and reward them their doings.
For they shall eat, and not have enough:
   they shall commit whoredom, and shall not increase:
   because they have left off to take heed to the Lord...

Come, and let us return unto the Lord:
   for he hath torn,
and he will heal us; he hath smitten,
   and he will bind us up.
After two days will he revive us:
   in the third day he will raise us up,
   and we shall live in his sight.
Then shall we know, if we follow on to know the Lord:
   his going forth is prepared as the morning;

and he shall come unto us as the rain,
    as the latter and former rain unto the earth.

O Ephraim, what shall I do unto thee?
    O Judah, what shall I do unto thee?
for your goodness is as a morning cloud,
    and as the early dew it goeth away.
Therefore have I hewed them by the prophets;
    I have slain them by the words of my mouth:
    and thy judgments are as the light that goeth forth.
For I desired mercy, and not sacrifice;
    and the knowledge of God more than burnt offerings.
But they like men have transgressed the covenant:
    there have they dealt treacherously against me…

Set the trumpet to thy mouth.
He shall come as an eagle against the house of the Lord,
    because they have transgressed my covenant,
    and trespassed against my law.
Israel shall cry unto me,
    My God, we know thee.
Israel hath cast off the thing that is good:
    the enemy shall pursue him.
They have set up kings, but not by me:
    they have made princes, and I knew it not:
of their silver and their gold have they made them idols,
    that they may be cut off.
Thy calf, O Samaria, hath cast thee off;
    mine anger is kindled against them:
    how long will it be ere they attain to innocency?
For from Israel was it also:
    the workman made it;
therefore it is not God:
    but the calf of Samaria shall be broken in pieces.

For they have sown the wind,
    and they shall reap the whirlwind:
it hath no stalk; the bud shall yield no meal:
    if so be it yield, the strangers shall swallow it up.

GOD'S LOVE FOR ISRAEL
Hosea 11:1–9

When Israel was a child, then I loved him,
    and called my son out of Egypt.
As they called them,
    so they went from them:
they sacrificed unto Baalim,
    and burned incense to graven images.
I taught Ephraim also to go,
    taking them by their arms;
    but they knew not that I healed them.
I drew them with cords of a man, with bands of love:
    and I was to them as they that take off the yoke on their jaws,
    and I laid meat unto them.

He shall not return into the land of Egypt,
    but the Assyrian shall be his king,
    because they refused to return.
And the sword shall abide on his cities,
    and shall consume his branches, and devour them,
    because of their own counsels.
And my people are bent to backsliding from me:
    though they called them to the most High,
    none at all would exalt him.

How shall I give thee up, Ephraim?
    how shall I deliver thee, Israel?
how shall I make thee as Admah?
    how shall I set thee as Zeboim?
mine heart is turned within me,
    my repentings are kindled together.
I will not execute the fierceness of mine anger,
    I will not return to destroy Ephraim:
for I am God, and not man;
    the Holy One in the midst of thee:
    and I will not enter into the city.

ISRAEL RETURNS TO GOD
Hosea 14

O Israel, return unto the Lord thy God;
    for thou hast fallen by thine iniquity.
Take with you words, and turn to the Lord:
    say unto him,
Take away all iniquity, and receive us graciously:
    so will we render the calves of our lips.
Asshur shall not save us; we will not ride upon horses:
    neither will we say any more to the work of our hands,
Ye are our gods:
    for in thee the fatherless findeth mercy.

I will heal their backsliding, I will love them freely:
    for mine anger is turned away from him.
I will be as the dew unto Israel:
    he shall grow as the lily,
    and cast forth his roots as Lebanon.
His branches shall spread,
    and his beauty shall be as the olive tree,
    and his smell as Lebanon.
They that dwell under his shadow shall return;
    they shall revive as the corn, and grow as the vine:
    the scent thereof shall be as the wine of Lebanon.
Ephraim shall say, What have I to do any more with idols?
    I have heard him, and observed him:
I am like a green fir tree.
    From me is thy fruit found.
Who is wise, and he shall understand these things?
    prudent, and he shall know them?
for the ways of the Lord are right,
    and the just shall walk in them:
    but the transgressors shall fall therein.

First Isaiah

A SINFUL NATION
Isaiah 1:1–20

The vision of Isaiah the son of Amoz, which he saw concerning Judah and Jerusalem in the days of Uzziah, Jotham, Ahaz, and Hezekiah, kings of Judah.

Hear, O heavens, and give ear, O earth:
　　for the Lord hath spoken,
I have nourished and brought up children,
　　and they have rebelled against me.
The ox knoweth his owner, and the ass his master's crib:
　　but Israel doth not know, my people doth not consider.

Ah sinful nation, a people laden with iniquity,
　　a seed of evildoers, children that are corrupters:
they have forsaken the Lord,
　　they have provoked the Holy One of Israel unto anger,
　　they are gone away backward.
Why should ye be stricken any more?
　　ye will revolt more and more:
the whole head is sick,
　　and the whole heart faint.
From the sole of the foot even unto the head
　　there is no soundness in it;
　　but wounds, and bruises, and putrifying sores:
they have not been closed, neither bound up,
　　neither mollified with ointment.
Your country is desolate, your cities are burned with fire:
　　your land, strangers devour it in your presence,
　　and it is desolate, as overthrown by strangers.
And the daughter of Zion is left as a cottage in a vineyard,
　　as a lodge in a garden of cucumbers, as a besieged city.

Except the Lord of hosts had left unto us a very small remnant,
    we should have been as Sodom,
    and we should have been like unto Gomorrah.
Hear the word of the Lord, ye rulers of Sodom;
    give ear unto the law of our God, ye people of Gomorrah.
To what purpose is the multitude of your sacrifices unto me?
      saith the Lord:
I am full of the burnt offerings of rams,
    and the fat of fed beasts;
and I delight not in the blood of bullocks,
    or of lambs, or of he goats.
When ye come to appear before me,
    who hath required this at your hand, to tread my courts?
Bring no more vain oblations;
    incense is an abomination unto me;
the new moons and sabbaths, the calling of assemblies,
    I cannot away with; it is iniquity, even the solemn meeting.
Your new moons and your appointed feasts my soul hateth:
    they are a trouble unto me; I am weary to bear them.
And when ye spread forth your hands,
    I will hide mine eyes from you:
yea, when ye make many prayers, I will not hear:
    your hands are full of blood.
Wash you, make you clean;
    put away the evil of your doings from before mine eyes;
    cease to do evil;
Learn to do well; seek judgment, relieve the oppressed,
    judge the fatherless, plead for the widow.
Come now, and let us reason together,
      saith the Lord:
though your sins be as scarlet,
    they shall be as white as snow;
though they be red like crimson,
    they shall be as wool.
If ye be willing and obedient, ye shall eat the good of the land:
But if ye refuse and rebel, ye shall be devoured with the sword:
    for the mouth of the Lord hath spoken it.

LAMENT FOR JERUSALEM
Isaiah 1:21–31

How is the faithful city become an harlot!
    it was full of judgment;
righteousness lodged in it;
    but now murderers.
Thy silver is become dross,
    thy wine mixed with water:
Thy princes are rebellious,
    and companions of thieves:
every one loveth gifts,
    and followeth after rewards:
they judge not the fatherless,
    neither doth the cause of the widow come unto them.
Therefore saith the Lord, the Lord of hosts,
    the mighty One of Israel,
Ah, I will ease me of mine adversaries,
    and avenge me of mine enemies:
And I will turn my hand upon thee,
    and purely purge away thy dross, and take away all thy tin:
And I will restore thy judges as at the first,
    and thy counsellors as at the beginning:
afterward thou shalt be called,
    The city of righteousness, the faithful city.
Zion shall be redeemed with judgment,
    and her converts with righteousness.
And the destruction of the transgressors
    and of the sinners shall be together,
    and they that forsake the Lord shall be consumed.
For they shall be ashamed of the oaks which ye have desired,
    and ye shall be confounded for the gardens that ye have chosen.
For ye shall be as an oak whose leaf fadeth,
    and as a garden that hath no water.
And the strong shall be as tow,
    and the maker of it as a spark,
and they shall both burn together,
    and none shall quench them.

PEACE ON EARTH
Isaiah 2:1–5

The word that Isaiah the son of Amoz saw concerning Judah and Jerusalem.

And it shall come to pass in the last days,
    that the mountain of the Lord's house
shall be established in the top of the mountains,
    and shall be exalted above the hills;
    and all nations shall flow unto it.

And many people shall go and say, Come ye,
    and let us go up to the mountain of the Lord,
    to the house of the God of Jacob;
and he will teach us of his ways,
    and we will walk in his paths:
for out of Zion shall go forth the law,
    and the word of the Lord from Jerusalem.
And he shall judge among the nations,
    and shall rebuke many people:
and they shall beat their swords into plowshares,
    and their spears into pruninghooks:
nation shall not lift up sword against nation,
    neither shall they learn war any more.

O house of Jacob, come ye,
    and let us walk in the light of the Lord.

GLORY TO GOD
Isaiah 2:11–21

The lofty looks of man shall be humbled,
    and the haughtiness of men shall be bowed down,
    and the Lord alone shall be exalted in that day.
For the day of the Lord of hosts
    shall be upon every one that is proud and lofty,

and upon every one that is lifted up;
    and he shall be brought low:
And upon all the cedars of Lebanon,
    that are high and lifted up,
    and upon all the oaks of Bashan,
And upon all the high mountains,
    and upon all the hills that are lifted up,
And upon every high tower,
    and upon every fenced wall,
And upon all the ships of Tarshish,
    and upon all pleasant pictures.
And the loftiness of man shall be bowed down,
    and the haughtiness of men shall be made low:
    and the Lord alone shall be exalted in that day.
And the idols he shall utterly abolish.
And they shall go into the holes of the rocks,
    and into the caves of the earth, for fear of the Lord,
and for the glory of his majesty,
    when he ariseth to shake terribly the earth.
In that day a man shall cast his idols of silver, and his idols of gold,
    which they made each one for himself to worship,
    to the moles and to the bats;
To go into the clefts of the rocks,
    and into the tops of the ragged rocks, for fear of the Lord,
and for the glory of his majesty,
    when he ariseth to shake terribly the earth.

JUDGMENT ON JERUSALEM
Isaiah 3:13 – 4:6

The Lord standeth up to plead,
    and standeth to judge the people.
The Lord will enter into judgment
    with the ancients of his people, and the princes thereof:
for ye have eaten up the vineyard;
    the spoil of the poor is in your houses.

What mean ye that ye beat my people to pieces,
    and grind the faces of the poor?
        saith the Lord God of hosts.

Moreover the Lord saith,

Because the daughters of Zion are haughty,
    and walk with stretched forth necks and wanton eyes,
walking and mincing as they go,
    and making a tinkling with their feet:
Therefore the Lord will smite with a scab
    the crown of the head of the daughters of Zion,
    and the Lord will discover their secret parts.

In that day the Lord will take away the bravery of their tinkling ornaments about their feet, and their cauls, and their round tires like the moon, the chains, and the bracelets, and the mufflers, the bonnets, and the ornaments of the legs, and the headbands, and the tablets, and the earrings, the rings, and nose jewels, the changeable suits of apparel, and the mantles, and the wimples, and the crisping pins, the glasses, and the fine linen, and the hoods, and the vails.

And it shall come to pass,
    that instead of sweet smell there shall be stink;
    and instead of a girdle a rent;
and instead of well set hair baldness;
    and instead of a stomacher a girding of sackcloth;
    and burning instead of beauty.
Thy men shall fall by the sword,
    and thy mighty in the war.
And her gates shall lament and mourn;
    and she being desolate shall sit upon the ground.

And in that day seven women shall take hold of one man, saying, We will eat our own bread, and wear our own apparel: only let us be called by thy name, to take away our reproach.

In that day shall the branch of the Lord be beautiful and glorious, and the fruit of the earth shall be excellent and comely for them that are escaped of Israel. And it shall come to pass, that he that is left in Zion, and he that remaineth in Jerusalem, shall be called holy, even every one that is written among the living in Jerusalem: When the Lord shall have washed away the filth of the daughters of Zion, and shall have purged the blood of Jerusalem from the midst thereof by the spirit of judgment, and by the spirit of burning. And the Lord will create upon every dwelling place of mount Zion, and upon her assemblies, a cloud and smoke by day, and the shining of a flaming fire by night: for upon all the glory shall be a defence. And there shall be a tabernacle for a shadow in the daytime from the heat, and for a place of refuge, and for a covert from storm and from rain.

THE SONG OF THE VINEYARD
Isaiah 5:1–7

Now will I sing to my wellbeloved a song of my beloved touching his vineyard.

My wellbeloved hath a vineyard in a very fruitful hill:
And he fenced it, and gathered out the stones thereof,
    and planted it with the choicest vine,
and built a tower in the midst of it,
    and also made a winepress therein:
and he looked that it should bring forth grapes,
    and it brought forth wild grapes.

And now, O inhabitants of Jerusalem, and men of Judah,
    judge, I pray you, betwixt me and my vineyard.
What could have been done more to my vineyard,
    that I have not done in it?
wherefore, when I looked that it should bring forth grapes,
    brought it forth wild grapes?

And now go to; I will tell you
    what I will do to my vineyard:
I will take away the hedge thereof,
    and it shall be eaten up;
and break down the wall thereof,
    and it shall be trodden down:

And I will lay it waste: it shall not be pruned, nor digged;
    but there shall come up briers and thorns:
I will also command the clouds
    that they rain no rain upon it.

For the vineyard of the Lord of hosts is the house of Israel,
    and the men of Judah his pleasant plant:
and he looked for judgment, but behold oppression;
    for righteousness, but behold a cry.

WOES AND JUDGMENTS
Isaiah 5:8–30

Woe unto them that join house to house,
    that lay field to field, till there be no place,
    that they may be placed alone in the midst of the earth!

In mine ears said the Lord of hosts,

Of a truth many houses shall be desolate,
    even great and fair, without inhabitant.
Yea, ten acres of vineyard shall yield one bath,
    and the seed of an homer shall yield an ephah.

Woe unto them that rise up early in the morning,
    that they may follow strong drink;
that continue until night,
    till wine inflame them!
And the harp, and the viol, the tabret,
    and pipe, and wine, are in their feasts:
but they regard not the work of the Lord,
    neither consider the operation of his hands.
Therefore my people are gone into captivity,
    because they have no knowledge:
and their honourable men are famished,
    and their multitude dried up with thirst.
Therefore hell hath enlarged herself,
    and opened her mouth without measure:

and their glory, and their multitude, and their pomp,
  and he that rejoiceth, shall descend into it.
And the mean man shall be brought down,
  and the mighty man shall be humbled,
  and the eyes of the lofty shall be humbled:
But the Lord of hosts shall be exalted in judgment,
  and God that is holy shall be sanctified in righteousness.
Then shall the lambs feed after their manner,
  and the waste places of the fat ones shall strangers eat.

Woe unto them that draw iniquity with cords of vanity,
  and sin as it were with a cart rope:
That say, Let him make speed, and hasten his work,
  that we may see it:
and let the counsel of the Holy One of Israel draw nigh
  and come, that we may know it!

Woe unto them that call evil good, and good evil;
  that put darkness for light, and light for darkness;
  that put bitter for sweet, and sweet for bitter!

Woe unto them that are wise in their own eyes,
  and prudent in their own sight!

Woe unto them that are mighty to drink wine,
  and men of strength to mingle strong drink:
Which justify the wicked for reward,
  and take away the righteousness of the righteous from him!

Therefore as the fire devoureth the stubble,
  and the flame consumeth the chaff,
so their root shall be as rottenness,
  and their blossom shall go up as dust:
because they have cast away the law of the Lord of hosts,
  and despised the word of the Holy One of Israel.
Therefore is the anger of the Lord kindled against his people,
  and he hath stretched forth his hand against them,
  and hath smitten them:
and the hills did tremble,
  and their carcases were torn in the midst of the streets.

For all this his anger is not turned away,
  but his hand is stretched out still.

And he will lift up an ensign to the nations from far,
  and will hiss unto them from the end of the earth:
  and, behold, they shall come with speed swiftly:
None shall be weary nor stumble among them;
  none shall slumber nor sleep;
neither shall the girdle of their loins be loosed,
  nor the latchet of their shoes be broken:
Whose arrows are sharp, and all their bows bent,
  their horses' hoofs shall be counted like flint,
  and their wheels like a whirlwind:
Their roaring shall be like a lion,
  they shall roar like young lions:
yea, they shall roar, and lay hold of the prey,
  and shall carry it away safe,
   and none shall deliver it.
And in that day they shall roar against them
  like the roaring of the sea:
and if one look unto the land, behold darkness and sorrow,
  and the light is darkened in the heavens thereof.

ISAIAH'S VISION AND COMMISSION
Isaiah 6

In the year that king Uzziah died I saw also the Lord sitting upon a throne, high and lifted up, and his train filled the temple. Above it stood the seraphims: each one had six wings; with twain he covered his face, and with twain he covered his feet, and with twain he did fly. And one cried unto another, and said,

  Holy, holy, holy, is the Lord of hosts:
    the whole earth is full of his glory.

And the posts of the door moved at the voice of him that cried, and the house was filled with smoke.

Then said I, Woe is me! for I am undone; because I am a man of unclean lips, and I dwell in the midst of a people of unclean lips: for mine eyes have seen the King, the Lord of hosts.

Then flew one of the seraphims unto me, having a live coal in his hand, which he had taken with the tongs from off the altar: and he laid it upon my mouth, and said, Lo, this hath touched thy lips; and thine iniquity is taken away, and thy sin purged. Also I heard the voice of the Lord, saying, Whom shall I send, and who will go for us? Then said I, Here am I; send me. And he said, Go, and tell this people,

Hear ye indeed, but understand not;
    and see ye indeed, but perceive not.
Make the heart of this people fat,
    and make their ears heavy,
    and shut their eyes;
lest they see with their eyes, and hear with their ears,
    and understand with their heart, and convert, and be healed.

Then said I, Lord, how long? And he answered,

Until the cities be wasted without inhabitant,
    and the houses without man,
    and the land be utterly desolate,
And the Lord have removed men far away,
    and there be a great forsaking in the midst of the land.
But yet in it shall be a tenth, and it shall return,
    and shall be eaten:
as a teil tree, and as an oak, whose substance is in them,
    when they cast their leaves:
    so the holy seed shall be the substance thereof.

THE SIGN OF IMMANUEL
Isaiah 7

And it came to pass in the days of Ahaz the son of Jotham, the son of Uzziah, king of Judah, that Rezin the king of Syria, and Pekah the son of Remaliah, king of Israel, went up toward Jerusalem to war against it, but could not prevail against it.

And it was told the house of David, saying, Syria is confederate with Ephraim. And his heart was moved, and the heart of his people, as the trees of the wood are moved with the wind.

Then said the Lord unto Isaiah, Go forth now to meet Ahaz, thou, and Shearjashub thy son, at the end of the conduit of the upper pool in the highway of the fuller's field; and say unto him, Take heed, and be quiet; fear not, neither be fainthearted for the two tails of these smoking firebrands, for the fierce anger of Rezin with Syria, and of the son of Remaliah. Because Syria, Ephraim, and the son of Remaliah, have taken evil counsel against thee, saying, Let us go up against Judah, and vex it, and let us make a breach therein for us, and set a king in the midst of it, even the son of Tabeal: thus saith the Lord God,

It shall not stand, neither shall it come to pass.
For the head of Syria is Damascus,
    and the head of Damascus is Rezin;
and within threescore and five years shall Ephraim be broken,
    that it be not a people.
And the head of Ephraim is Samaria,
    and the head of Samaria is Remaliah's son.
If ye will not believe,
    surely ye shall not be established.

Moreover the Lord spake again unto Ahaz, saying, Ask thee a sign of the Lord thy God; ask it either in the depth, or in the height above.

But Ahaz said, I will not ask, neither will I tempt the Lord.

And he said, Hear ye now, O house of David; is it a small thing for you to weary men, but will ye weary my God also? Therefore the Lord himself shall give you a sign; behold, a virgin shall conceive, and bear a son, and shall call his name Immanuel. Butter and honey shall he eat, that he may know to refuse the evil, and choose the good. For before the child shall know to refuse the evil, and choose the good, the land that thou abhorrest shall be forsaken of both her kings. The Lord shall bring upon thee, and upon thy people, and upon thy father's house, days that have not come, from the day that Ephraim departed from Judah; even the king of Assyria.

And it shall come to pass in that day, that the Lord shall hiss for the fly that is in the uttermost part of the rivers of Egypt, and for the bee that is in the land of Assyria. And they shall come, and shall rest all of them in the desolate valleys, and in the holes of the rocks, and upon all thorns, and upon all bushes. In the same day shall the Lord shave with a razor that is hired, namely, by them beyond the river, by the king of Assyria, the head, and the hair of the feet: and it shall also consume the beard. And it shall come to pass in that day, that a man shall nourish a young cow, and two sheep; and it shall come to pass, for the abundance of milk that they shall give he shall eat butter: for butter and honey shall every one eat that is left in the land. And it shall come to pass in that day, that every place shall be, where there were a thousand vines at a thousand silverlings, it shall even be for briers and thorns. With arrows and with bows shall men come thither; because all the land shall become briers and thorns. And on all hills that shall be digged with the mattock, there shall not come thither the fear of briers and thorns: but it shall be for the sending forth of oxen, and for the treading of lesser cattle.

THE PRINCE OF PEACE
Isaiah 9:2–7

The people that walked in darkness have seen a great light:
    they that dwell in the land of the shadow of death,
    upon them hath the light shined.
Thou hast multiplied the nation, and not increased the joy:
    they joy before thee according to the joy in harvest,
    and as men rejoice when they divide the spoil.
For thou hast broken the yoke of his burden,
    and the staff of his shoulder, the rod of his oppressor,
    as in the day of Midian.
For every battle of the warrior is with confused noise,
    and garments rolled in blood;
    but this shall be with burning and fuel of fire.
For unto us a child is born, unto us a son is given:
    and the government shall be upon his shoulder:
    and his name shall be called

Wonderful, Counsellor,
The mighty God, The everlasting Father,
The Prince of Peace.
Of the increase of his government and peace
there shall be no end,
upon the throne of David, and upon his kingdom,
to order it, and to establish it with judgment
and with justice from henceforth even for ever.
The zeal of the Lord of hosts will perform this.

THE PEACEABLE KINGDOM
Isaiah 11:1–9

And there shall come forth a rod out of the stem of Jesse,
and a Branch shall grow out of his roots:
And the spirit of the Lord shall rest upon him,
the spirit of wisdom and understanding,
the spirit of counsel and might,
the spirit of knowledge and of the fear of the Lord;
And shall make him of quick understanding in the fear of the Lord:
and he shall not judge after the sight of his eyes,
neither reprove after the hearing of his ears:
But with righteousness shall he judge the poor,
and reprove with equity for the meek of the earth:
and he shall smite the earth with the rod of his mouth,
and with the breath of his lips shall he slay the wicked.
And righteousness shall be the girdle of his loins,
and faithfulness the girdle of his reins.

The wolf also shall dwell with the lamb,
and the leopard shall lie down with the kid;
and the calf and the young lion and the fatling together;
and a little child shall lead them.
And the cow and the bear shall feed;
their young ones shall lie down together:
and the lion shall eat straw like the ox.

And the sucking child shall play on the hole of the asp,
    and the weaned child shall put his hand on the cockatrice' den.
They shall not hurt nor destroy in all my holy mountain:
    for the earth shall be full of the knowledge of the Lord,
    as the waters cover the sea.

THE FALL OF THE KING OF BABYLON
Isaiah 14:1–23

For the Lord will have mercy on Jacob,
    and will yet choose Israel, and set them in their own land:
and the strangers shall be joined with them,
    and they shall cleave to the house of Jacob.
And the people shall take them,
    and bring them to their place:
and the house of Israel shall possess them in the land of the Lord
    for servants and handmaids:
and they shall take them captives, whose captives they were;
    and they shall rule over their oppressors.

And it shall come to pass in the day that the Lord shall give thee rest
from thy sorrow, and from thy fear, and from the hard bondage
wherein thou wast made to serve, that thou shalt take up this proverb
against the king of Babylon, and say,

How hath the oppressor ceased! the golden city ceased!
The Lord hath broken the staff of the wicked,
    and the sceptre of the rulers.
He who smote the people in wrath with a continual stroke,
    he that ruled the nations in anger,
    is persecuted, and none hindereth.
The whole earth is at rest, and is quiet:
    they break forth into singing.
Yea, the fir trees rejoice at thee,
    and the cedars of Lebanon, saying,
Since thou art laid down,
    no feller is come up against us.

Hell from beneath is moved for thee to meet thee at thy coming:
  it stirreth up the dead for thee,
  even all the chief ones of the earth;
it hath raised up from their thrones
  all the kings of the nations.
All they shall speak and say unto thee,
  Art thou also become weak as we?
  art thou become like unto us?

Thy pomp is brought down to the grave,
  and the noise of thy viols:
the worm is spread under thee,
  and the worms cover thee.
How art thou fallen from heaven,
  O Lucifer, son of the morning!
how art thou cut down to the ground,
  which didst weaken the nations!

For thou hast said in thine heart,
  I will ascend into heaven,
I will exalt my throne
  above the stars of God:
I will sit also upon the mount of the congregation,
  in the sides of the north:
I will ascend above the heights of the clouds;
  I will be like the most High.
Yet thou shalt be brought down to hell,
  to the sides of the pit.

They that see thee shall narrowly look upon thee,
  and consider thee, saying,
Is this the man that made the earth to tremble,
  that did shake kingdoms;
That made the world as a wilderness,
  and destroyed the cities thereof;
  that opened not the house of his prisoners?

All the kings of the nations, even all of them, lie in glory,
  every one in his own house.

But thou art cast out of thy grave
  like an abominable branch,
and as the raiment of those that are slain,
  thrust through with a sword,
that go down to the stones of the pit;
  as a carcase trodden under feet.
Thou shalt not be joined with them in burial,
  because thou hast destroyed thy land, and slain thy people:
  the seed of evildoers shall never be renowned.
Prepare slaughter for his children for the iniquity of their fathers;
  that they do not rise, nor possess the land,
  nor fill the face of the world with cities.

For I will rise up against them,
    saith the Lord of hosts,
  and cut off from Babylon the name, and remnant,
  and son, and nephew,
    saith the Lord.

I will also make it a possession for the bittern,
  and pools of water:
and I will sweep it with the besom of destruction,
    saith the Lord of hosts.

THE DAY OF PUNISHMENT
Isaiah 24

Behold, the Lord maketh the earth empty,
  and maketh it waste, and turneth it upside down,
  and scattereth abroad the inhabitants thereof.
And it shall be, as with the people, so with the priest;
  as with the servant, so with his master;
  as with the maid, so with her mistress;
  as with the buyer, so with the seller;
  as with the lender, so with the borrower;
  as with the taker of usury, so with the giver of usury to him.

The land shall be utterly emptied, and utterly spoiled:
    for the Lord hath spoken this word.

The earth mourneth and fadeth away,
    the world languisheth and fadeth away,
    the haughty people of the earth do languish.
The earth also is defiled under the inhabitants thereof;
    because they have transgressed the laws,
    changed the ordinance, broken the everlasting covenant.
Therefore hath the curse devoured the earth,
    and they that dwell therein are desolate:
therefore the inhabitants of the earth are burned,
    and few men left.
The new wine mourneth, the vine languisheth,
    all the merryhearted do sigh.
The mirth of tabrets ceaseth,
    the noise of them that rejoice endeth,
    the joy of the harp ceaseth.
They shall not drink wine with a song;
    strong drink shall be bitter to them that drink it.
The city of confusion is broken down:
    every house is shut up, that no man may come in.
There is a crying for wine in the streets;
    all joy is darkened, the mirth of the land is gone.
In the city is left desolation,
    and the gate is smitten with destruction.
When thus it shall be in the midst of the land among the people,
    there shall be as the shaking of an olive tree,
    and as the gleaning grapes when the vintage is done.

They shall lift up their voice,
    they shall sing for the majesty of the Lord,
    they shall cry aloud from the sea.
Wherefore glorify ye the Lord in the fires,
    even the name of the Lord God of Israel in the isles of the sea.
From the uttermost part of the earth have we heard songs,
    even glory to the righteous.

But I said, My leanness, my leanness, woe unto me!
  the treacherous dealers have dealt treacherously;
  yea, the treacherous dealers have dealt very treacherously.
Fear, and the pit, and the snare, are upon thee,
  O inhabitant of the earth.
And it shall come to pass,
  that he who fleeth from the noise of the fear
  shall fall into the pit;
and he that cometh up out of the midst of the pit
  shall be taken in the snare:
for the windows from on high are open,
  and the foundations of the earth do shake.
The earth is utterly broken down,
  the earth is clean dissolved,
  the earth is moved exceedingly.
The earth shall reel to and fro like a drunkard,
  and shall be removed like a cottage;
and the transgression thereof shall be heavy upon it;
  and it shall fall, and not rise again.

And it shall come to pass in that day, that the Lord
  shall punish the host of the high ones that are on high,
  and the kings of the earth upon the earth.
And they shall be gathered together,
  as prisoners are gathered in the pit,
  and shall be shut up in the prison,
  and after many days shall they be visited.
Then the moon shall be confounded, and the sun ashamed,
  when the Lord of hosts shall reign in mount Zion,
  and in Jerusalem, and before his ancients gloriously.

A PRAYER OF THANKSGIVING
Isaiah 25:1–5

O Lord, thou art my God; I will exalt thee,
  I will praise thy name;

For thou hast made of a city an heap;
    of a defenced city a ruin:
a palace of strangers to be no city;
    it shall never be built.
Therefore shall the strong people glorify thee,
    the city of the terrible nations shall fear thee.
For thou hast been a strength to the poor,
    a strength to the needy in his distress,
a refuge from the storm,
    a shadow from the heat,
when the blast of the terrible ones
    is as a storm against the wall.
Thou shalt bring down the noise of strangers,
    as the heat in a dry place;
even the heat with the shadow of a cloud:
    the branch of the terrible ones shall be brought low.

THE MESSIANIC FEAST
Isaiah 25:6–9

And in this mountain shall the Lord of hosts
    make unto all people a feast of fat things,
a feast of wines on the lees, of fat things full of marrow,
    of wines on the lees well refined.
And he will destroy in this mountain
    the face of the covering cast over all people,
    and the vail that is spread over all nations.
He will swallow up death in victory;
    and the Lord God will wipe away tears from off all faces;
and the rebuke of his people
    shall he take away from off all the earth:
    for the Lord hath spoken it.
And it shall be said in that day, Lo, this is our God;
    we have waited for him, and he will save us:
this is the Lord; we have waited for him,
    we will be glad and rejoice in his salvation.

A VICTORY SONG
Isaiah 26:1–19

In that day shall this song be sung in the land of Judah;

We have a strong city;
  salvation will God appoint for walls and bulwarks.
Open ye the gates,
  that the righteous nation which keepeth the truth may enter in.
Thou wilt keep him in perfect peace,
  whose mind is stayed on thee: because he trusteth in thee.
Trust ye in the Lord for ever:
  for in the Lord Jehovah is everlasting strength:
For he bringeth down them that dwell on high;
  the lofty city, he layeth it low;
he layeth it low, even to the ground;
  he bringeth it even to the dust.
The foot shall tread it down, even the feet of the poor,
  and the steps of the needy.

The way of the just is uprightness:
  thou, most upright, dost weigh the path of the just.
Yea, in the way of thy judgments, O Lord,
  have we waited for thee;
the desire of our soul is to thy name,
  and to the remembrance of thee.
With my soul have I desired thee in the night;
  yea, with my spirit within me will I seek thee early:
for when thy judgments are in the earth,
  the inhabitants of the world will learn righteousness.
Let favour be shewed to the wicked,
  yet will he not learn righteousness:
in the land of uprightness will he deal unjustly,
  and will not behold the majesty of the Lord.
Lord, when thy hand is lifted up, they will not see:
  but they shall see,
and be ashamed for their envy at the people;
  yea, the fire of thine enemies shall devour them.

Lord, thou wilt ordain peace for us:
  for thou also hast wrought all our works in us.
O Lord our God, other lords beside thee have had dominion over us:
  but by thee only will we make mention of thy name.
They are dead, they shall not live;
   they are deceased, they shall not rise:
therefore hast thou visited and destroyed them,
  and made all their memory to perish.
Thou hast increased the nation, O Lord,
  thou hast increased the nation:
thou art glorified:
  thou hadst removed it far unto all the ends of the earth.

Lord, in trouble have they visited thee,
  they poured out a prayer when thy chastening was upon them.
Like as a woman with child,
  that draweth near the time of her delivery,
is in pain, and crieth out in her pangs;
  so have we been in thy sight, O Lord.
We have been with child, we have been in pain,
  we have as it were brought forth wind;
we have not wrought any deliverance in the earth;
  neither have the inhabitants of the world fallen.

Thy dead men shall live,
  together with my dead body shall they arise.
Awake and sing, ye that dwell in dust:
  for thy dew is as the dew of herbs,
  and the earth shall cast out the dead.

THE RIGHTEOUS KINGDOM
Isaiah 32:1–8

Behold, a king shall reign in righteousness,
  and princes shall rule in judgment.
And a man shall be as an hiding place from the wind,
  and a covert from the tempest;

as rivers of water in a dry place,
   as the shadow of a great rock in a weary land.

And the eyes of them that see shall not be dim,
   and the ears of them that hear shall hearken.
The heart also of the rash shall understand knowledge,
   and the tongue of the stammerers shall be ready to speak plainly.
The vile person shall be no more called liberal,
   nor the churl said to be bountiful.
For the vile person will speak villany, and his heart will work iniquity,
   to practise hypocrisy, and to utter error against the Lord,
to make empty the soul of the hungry,
   and he will cause the drink of the thirsty to fail.
The instruments also of the churl are evil:
   he deviseth wicked devices to destroy the poor with lying words,
   even when the needy speaketh right.
But the liberal deviseth liberal things;
   and by liberal things shall he stand.

THE JOY OF THE REDEEMED
Isaiah 35

The wilderness and the solitary place shall be glad for them;
   and the desert shall rejoice, and blossom as the rose.
It shall blossom abundantly,
   and rejoice even with joy and singing:
the glory of Lebanon shall be given unto it,
   the excellency of Carmel and Sharon,
they shall see the glory of the Lord,
   and the excellency of our God.

Strengthen ye the weak hands,
   and confirm the feeble knees.
Say to them that are of a fearful heart, Be strong, fear not:
   behold, your God will come with vengeance,
even God with a recompence;
   he will come and save you.

Then the eyes of the blind shall be opened,
  and the ears of the deaf shall be unstopped.
Then shall the lame man leap as an hart,
  and the tongue of the dumb sing:
for in the wilderness shall waters break out,
  and streams in the desert.
And the parched ground shall become a pool,
  and the thirsty land springs of water:
in the habitation of dragons,
    where each lay, shall be grass with reeds and rushes.

And an highway shall be there, and a way,
  and it shall be called The way of holiness;
the unclean shall not pass over it;
  but it shall be for those:
the wayfaring men, though fools,
  shall not err therein.
No lion shall be there,
  nor any ravenous beast shall go up thereon,
it shall not be found there;
  but the redeemed shall walk there:
And the ransomed of the Lord shall return, and come to Zion
  with songs and everlasting joy upon their heads:
they shall obtain joy and gladness,
  and sorrow and sighing shall flee away.

Micah

JUDGMENT ON SAMARIA AND JERUSALEM
Micah 1:1–10

The word of the Lord that came to Micah the Morasthite in the days of Jotham, Ahaz, and Hezekiah, kings of Judah, which he saw concerning Samaria and Jerusalem.

Hear, all ye people;
   hearken, O earth, and all that therein is:
and let the Lord God be witness against you,
   the Lord from his holy temple.
For, behold, the Lord cometh forth out of his place,
   and will come down,
   and tread upon the high places of the earth.
And the mountains shall be molten under him,
   and the valleys shall be cleft, as wax before the fire,
   and as the waters that are poured down a steep place.
For the transgression of Jacob is all this,
   and for the sins of the house of Israel.
What is the transgression of Jacob?
   is it not Samaria?
   and what are the high places of Judah?
   are they not Jerusalem?

Therefore I will make Samaria as an heap of the field,
   and as plantings of a vineyard:
and I will pour down the stones thereof into the valley,
   and I will discover the foundations thereof.
And all the graven images thereof shall be beaten to pieces,
   and all the hires thereof shall be burned with the fire,
   and all the idols thereof will I lay desolate:
for she gathered it of the hire of an harlot,
   and they shall return to the hire of an harlot.

Therefore I will wail and howl,
    I will go stripped and naked:
I will make a wailing like the dragons,
    and mourning as the owls.
For her wound is incurable;
    for it is come unto Judah;
he is come unto the gate of my people,
    even to Jerusalem.
Declare ye it not at Gath, weep ye not at all:
    in the house of Aphrah roll thyself in the dust.

WOE TO THE EVILDOERS
Micah 2:1–5

Woe to them that devise iniquity,
    and work evil upon their beds!
when the morning is light, they practise it,
    because it is in the power of their hand.
And they covet fields, and take them by violence;
    and houses, and take them away:
so they oppress a man and his house,
    even a man and his heritage.

Therefore thus saith the Lord;

Behold, against this family do I devise an evil,
    from which ye shall not remove your necks;
neither shall ye go haughtily:
    for this time is evil.
In that day shall one take up a parable against you,
    and lament with a doleful lamentation, and say,
We be utterly spoiled:
    he hath changed the portion of my people:
how hath he removed it from me!
    turning away he hath divided our fields.

Therefore thou shalt have none that shall cast a cord by lot
    in the congregation of the Lord.

THE RULER FROM BETHLEHEM
Micah 5:1–4

Now gather thyself in troops,
    O daughter of troops:
he hath laid siege against us:
    they shall smite the judge of Israel with a rod upon the cheek.

But thou, Bethlehem Ephratah,
    though thou be little among the thousands of Judah,
yet out of thee shall he come forth unto me
    that is to be ruler in Israel;
whose goings forth have been from of old,
    from everlasting.
Therefore will he give them up,
    until the time that she which travaileth hath brought forth:
then the remnant of his brethren
    shall return unto the children of Israel.

And he shall stand and feed in the strength of the Lord,
    in the majesty of the name of the Lord his God;
and they shall abide:
    for now shall he be great unto the ends of the earth.

GOD PLEADS WITH HIS PEOPLE
Micah 6:1–8

Hear ye now what the Lord saith;

Arise, contend thou before the mountains,
    and let the hills hear thy voice.
Hear ye, O mountains, the Lord's controversy,
    and ye strong foundations of the earth:
for the Lord hath a controversy with his people,
    and he will plead with Israel.

O my people, what have I done unto thee?
    and wherein have I wearied thee? testify against me.

For I brought thee up out of the land of Egypt,
    and redeemed thee out of the house of servants;
    and I sent before thee Moses, Aaron, and Miriam.
O my people, remember now
    what Balak king of Moab consulted,
and what Balaam the son of Beor answered him
    from Shittim unto Gilgal;
that ye may know the righteousness of the Lord.

Wherewith shall I come before the Lord,
    and bow myself before the high God?
shall I come before him with burnt offerings,
    with calves of a year old?
Will the Lord be pleased with thousands of rams,
    or with ten thousands of rivers of oil?
shall I give my firstborn for my transgression,
    the fruit of my body for the sin of my soul?
He hath shewed thee, O man, what is good;
    and what doth the Lord require of thee,
but to do justly, and to love mercy,
    and to walk humbly with thy God?

A PRAYER
Micah 7:14–20

Feed thy people with thy rod,
    the flock of thine heritage,
which dwell solitarily in the wood,
    in the midst of Carmel:
let them feed in Bashan and Gilead,
    as in the days of old.

According to the days of thy coming out of the land of Egypt
    will I shew unto him marvellous things.

The nations shall see and be confounded at all their might:
    they shall lay their hand upon their mouth,
    their ears shall be deaf.

They shall lick the dust like a serpent,
    they shall move out of their holes like worms of the earth:
they shall be afraid of the Lord our God,
    and shall fear because of thee.
Who is a God like unto thee, that pardoneth iniquity,
    and passeth by the transgression of the remnant of his heritage?
he retaineth not his anger for ever,
    because he delighteth in mercy.
He will turn again,
    he will have compassion upon us;
he will subdue our iniquities;
    and thou wilt cast all their sins into the depths of the sea.
Thou wilt perform the truth to Jacob,
    and the mercy to Abraham,
which thou hast sworn unto our fathers
    from the days of old.

Zephaniah

THE DAY OF JUDGMENT
Zephaniah 1:1–3, 7–9, 14–18, 2:1–3

The word of the Lord which came unto Zephaniah the son of Cushi,
the son of Gedaliah, the son of Amariah, the son of Hizkiah, in the
days of Josiah the son of Amon, king of Judah.

I will utterly consume all things from off the land,
    saith the Lord.
I will consume man and beast;
I will consume the fowls of the heaven,
  and the fishes of the sea,
and the stumbling blocks with the wicked:
    and I will cut off man from off the land,
      saith the Lord…
Hold thy peace at the presence of the Lord God:
    for the day of the Lord is at hand:
for the Lord hath prepared a sacrifice,
    he hath bid his guests.
And it shall come to pass in the day of the Lord's sacrifice,
    that I will punish the princes, and the king's children,
    and all such as are clothed with strange apparel.
In the same day also will I punish all those
    that leap on the threshold,
    which fill their masters' houses with violence and deceit…

The great day of the Lord is near, it is near,
    and hasteth greatly, even the voice of the day of the Lord:
    the mighty man shall cry there bitterly.
That day is a day of wrath, a day of trouble and distress,
    a day of wasteness and desolation,
    a day of darkness and gloominess,
    a day of clouds and thick darkness,

A day of the trumpet and alarm against the fenced cities,
    and against the high towers.
And I will bring distress upon men,
    that they shall walk like blind men,
    because they have sinned against the Lord:
and their blood shall be poured out as dust,
    and their flesh as the dung.
Neither their silver nor their gold shall be able
    to deliver them in the day of the Lord's wrath;
but the whole land shall be devoured by the fire of his jealousy:
    for he shall make even a speedy riddance of all them
    that dwell in the land.

Gather yourselves together,
    yea, gather together, O nation not desired;
Before the decree bring forth, before the day pass as the chaff,
    before the fierce anger of the Lord come upon you,
    before the day of the Lord's anger come upon you.
Seek ye the Lord, all ye meek of the earth,
    which have wrought his judgment;
seek righteousness, seek meekness:
    it may be ye shall be hid in the day of the Lord's anger.

THE DAY OF SALVATION
Zephaniah 3:9–20

For then will I turn to the people a pure language,
    that they may all call upon the name of the Lord,
    to serve him with one consent.
From beyond the rivers of Ethiopia my suppliants,
    even the daughter of my dispersed, shall bring mine offering.
In that day shalt thou not be ashamed for all thy doings,
    wherein thou hast transgressed against me:
for then I will take away out of the midst of thee
    them that rejoice in thy pride,
and thou shalt no more be haughty
    because of my holy mountain.

I will also leave in the midst of thee an afflicted and poor people,
    and they shall trust in the name of the Lord.
The remnant of Israel shall not do iniquity, nor speak lies;
    neither shall a deceitful tongue be found in their mouth:
for they shall feed and lie down,
    and none shall make them afraid.

Sing, O daughter of Zion; shout, O Israel;
    be glad and rejoice with all the heart,
    O daughter of Jerusalem.
The Lord hath taken away thy judgments,
    he hath cast out thine enemy: the king of Israel,
even the Lord, is in the midst of thee:
    thou shalt not see evil any more.
In that day it shall be said to Jerusalem, Fear thou not:
    and to Zion, Let not thine hands be slack.
The Lord thy God in the midst of thee is mighty;
    he will save, he will rejoice over thee with joy;
he will rest in his love,
    he will joy over thee with singing.
I will gather them that are sorrowful for the solemn assembly,
    who are of thee, to whom the reproach of it was a burden.
Behold, at that time I will undo all that afflict thee:
    and I will save her that halteth,
    and gather her that was driven out;
and I will get them praise and fame in every land
    where they have been put to shame.
At that time will I bring you again,
    even in the time that I gather you:
for I will make you a name and a praise
    among all people of the earth,
when I turn back your captivity before your eyes,
      saith the Lord.

Nahum

GOD'S JUDGMENT ON NINEVEH
Nahum 1:1–10, 3:1–4, 18–19

The burden of Nineveh. The book of the vision of Nahum the Elkoshite.

God is jealous, and the Lord revengeth;
    the Lord revengeth, and is furious;
the Lord will take vengeance on his adversaries,
    and he reserveth wrath for his enemies.
The Lord is slow to anger, and great in power,
    and will not at all acquit the wicked:
the Lord hath his way in the whirlwind and in the storm,
    and the clouds are the dust of his feet.
He rebuketh the sea, and maketh it dry,
    and drieth up all the rivers:
Bashan languisheth, and Carmel,
    and the flower of Lebanon languisheth.
The mountains quake at him, and the hills melt,
    and the earth is burned at his presence,
    yea, the world, and all that dwell therein.
Who can stand before his indignation?
    and who can abide in the fierceness of his anger?
his fury is poured out like fire,
    and the rocks are thrown down by him.

The Lord is good, a strong hold in the day of trouble;
    and he knoweth them that trust in him.
But with an overrunning flood
    he will make an utter end of the place thereof,
    and darkness shall pursue his enemies.
What do ye imagine against the Lord?
    he will make an utter end:
    affliction shall not rise up the second time.

For while they be folden together as thorns,
    and while they are drunken as drunkards,
      they shall be devoured as stubble fully dry...

Woe to the bloody city! it is all full of lies and robbery;
    the prey departeth not;
The noise of a whip, and the noise of the rattling of the wheels,
    and of the pransing horses, and of the jumping chariots.
The horseman lifteth up both the bright sword
    and the glittering spear:
and there is a multitude of slain,
    and a great number of carcases;
and there is none end of their corpses;
    they stumble upon their corpses:
Because of the multitude of the whoredoms
    of the wellfavoured harlot, the mistress of witchcrafts,
that selleth nations through her whoredoms,
    and families through her witchcrafts...

Thy shepherds slumber, O king of Assyria:
    thy nobles shall dwell in the dust:
thy people is scattered upon the mountains,
    and no man gathereth them.
There is no healing of thy bruise;
    thy wound is grievous:
all that hear the bruit of thee shall clap the hands over thee:
    for upon whom hath not thy wickedness passed continually?

Habakkuk

HABAKKUK'S COMPLAINT
Habakkuk 1:1–4, 12–17, 2:1

The burden which Habakkuk the prophet did see.

O Lord, how long shall I cry,
    and thou wilt not hear!
even cry out unto thee of violence,
    and thou wilt not save!
Why dost thou shew me iniquity,
    and cause me to behold grievance?
for spoiling and violence are before me:
    and there are that raise up strife and contention.
Therefore the law is slacked,
    and judgment doth never go forth:
for the wicked doth compass about the righteous;
    therefore wrong judgment proceedeth...

Art thou not from everlasting,
    O Lord my God, mine Holy One? we shall not die.
O Lord, thou hast ordained them for judgment;
    and, O mighty God, thou hast established them for correction.
Thou art of purer eyes than to behold evil,
    and canst not look on iniquity:
wherefore lookest thou upon them that deal treacherously,
    and holdest thy tongue when the wicked
    devoureth the man that is more righteous than he?
And makest men as the fishes of the sea,
    as the creeping things, that have no ruler over them?
They take up all of them with the angle,
    they catch them in their net,
and gather them in their drag:
    therefore they rejoice and are glad.

Therefore they sacrifice unto their net,
    and burn incense unto their drag;
because by them their portion is fat,
    and their meat plenteous.
Shall they therefore empty their net,
    and not spare continually to slay the nations?

I will stand upon my watch, and set me upon the tower,
    and will watch to see what he will say unto me,
    and what I shall answer when I am reproved.

GOD'S ANSWER
Habakkuk 2:2–4, 9–14, 18–20

And the Lord answered me, and said,

Write the vision, and make it plain upon tables,
    that he may run that readeth it.
For the vision is yet for an appointed time,
    but at the end it shall speak, and not lie:
though it tarry, wait for it; because it will surely come,
    it will not tarry.
Behold, his soul which is lifted up is not upright in him:
    but the just shall live by his faith...

Woe to him that coveteth an evil covetousness to his house,
    that he may set his nest on high,
    that he may be delivered from the power of evil!
Thou hast consulted shame to thy house
    by cutting off many people, and hast sinned against thy soul.
For the stone shall cry out of the wall,
    and the beam out of the timber shall answer it.

Woe to him that buildeth a town with blood,
    and stablisheth a city by iniquity!
Behold, is it not of the Lord of hosts
    that the people shall labour in the very fire,
    and the people shall weary themselves for very vanity?

For the earth shall be filled
    with the knowledge of the glory of the Lord,
    as the waters cover the sea…

What profiteth the graven image
    that the maker thereof hath graven it;
the molten image, and a teacher of lies,
    that the maker of his work trusteth therein,
    to make dumb idols?
Woe unto him that saith to the wood, Awake;
    to the dumb stone, Arise, it shall teach!
Behold, it is laid over with gold and silver,
    and there is no breath at all in the midst of it.
But the Lord is in his holy temple:
    let all the earth keep silence before him.

HABAKKUK'S PRAYER
Habakkuk 3:2–19

O Lord, I have heard thy speech, and was afraid:
O Lord, revive thy work in the midst of the years,
    in the midst of the years make known;
    in wrath remember mercy.

God came from Teman,
    and the Holy One from mount Paran.
His glory covered the heavens,
    and the earth was full of his praise.
And his brightness was as the light;
    he had horns coming out of his hand:
    and there was the hiding of his power.
Before him went the pestilence,
    and burning coals went forth at his feet.
He stood, and measured the earth:
    he beheld, and drove asunder the nations;
and the everlasting mountains were scattered,
    the perpetual hills did bow: his ways are everlasting.

I saw the tents of Cushan in affliction:
   and the curtains of the land of Midian did tremble.
Was the Lord displeased against the rivers?
   was thine anger against the rivers?
was thy wrath against the sea,
   that thou didst ride upon thine horses
   and thy chariots of salvation?
Thy bow was made quite naked,
   according to the oaths of the tribes, even thy word.
Thou didst cleave the earth with rivers.
The mountains saw thee, and they trembled:
   the overflowing of the water passed by:
the deep uttered his voice,
   and lifted up his hands on high.

The sun and moon stood still in their habitation:
   at the light of thine arrows they went,
   and at the shining of thy glittering spear.
Thou didst march through the land in indignation,
   thou didst thresh the heathen in anger.
Thou wentest forth for the salvation of thy people,
   even for salvation with thine anointed;
thou woundedst the head out of the house of the wicked,
   by discovering the foundation unto the neck.
Thou didst strike through with his staves the head of his villages:
   they came out as a whirlwind to scatter me:
   their rejoicing was as to devour the poor secretly.
Thou didst walk through the sea with thine horses,
   through the heap of great waters.

When I heard, my belly trembled;
   my lips quivered at the voice:
rottenness entered into my bones, and I trembled in myself,
   that I might rest in the day of trouble:
when he cometh up unto the people,
   he will invade them with his troops.
Although the fig tree shall not blossom,
   neither shall fruit be in the vines;

the labour of the olive shall fail,
    and the fields shall yield no meat;
the flock shall be cut off from the fold,
    and there shall be no herd in the stalls:
Yet I will rejoice in the Lord,
    I will joy in the God of my salvation.

The Lord God is my strength,
    and he will make my feet like hinds' feet,
    and he will make me to walk upon mine high places.

Jeremiah

THE CALL OF JEREMIAH
Jeremiah 1

The words of Jeremiah the son of Hilkiah, of the priests that were in
Anathoth in the land of Benjamin: to whom the word of the Lord
came in the days of Josiah the son of Amon king of Judah, in the
thirteenth year of his reign. It came also in the days of Jehoiakim the
son of Josiah king of Judah, unto the end of the eleventh year of
Zedekiah the son of Josiah king of Judah, unto the carrying away of
Jerusalem captive in the fifth month.

Then the word of the Lord came unto me, saying,

Before I formed thee in the belly I knew thee;
    and before thou camest forth out of the womb I sanctified thee,
    and I ordained thee a prophet unto the nations.

Then said I, Ah, Lord God! behold, I cannot speak: for I am a child.
But the Lord said unto me, Say not, I am a child: for thou shalt go to
all that I shall send thee, and whatsoever I command thee thou shalt
speak. Be not afraid of their faces: for I am with thee to deliver thee,
saith the Lord.

Then the Lord put forth his hand, and touched my mouth. And the
Lord said unto me, Behold, I have put my words in thy mouth. See,
I have this day set thee over the nations and over the kingdoms, to
root out, and to pull down, and to destroy, and to throw down, to
build, and to plant.

Moreover the word of the Lord came unto me, saying, Jeremiah,
what seest thou? And I said, I see a rod of an almond tree. Then said
the Lord unto me, Thou hast well seen: for I will hasten my word to
perform it.

And the word of the Lord came unto me the second time, saying,
What seest thou? And I said, I see a seething pot; and the face thereof
is toward the north. Then the Lord said unto me, Out of the north an

evil shall break forth upon all the inhabitants of the land. For, lo, I will call all the families of the kingdoms of the north, saith the Lord; and they shall come, and they shall set every one his throne at the entering of the gates of Jerusalem, and against all the walls thereof round about, and against all the cities of Judah. And I will utter my judgments against them touching all their wickedness, who have forsaken me, and have burned incense unto other gods, and worshipped the works of their own hands. Thou therefore gird up thy loins, and arise, and speak unto them all that I command thee: be not dismayed at their faces, lest I confound thee before them. For, behold, I have made thee this day a defenced city, and an iron pillar, and brasen walls against the whole land, against the kings of Judah, against the princes thereof, against the priests thereof, and against the people of the land. And they shall fight against thee; but they shall not prevail against thee; for I am with thee, saith the Lord, to deliver thee.

JUDAH TURNS AWAY FROM GOD
Jeremiah 3:6–17

The Lord said also unto me in the days of Josiah the king, Hast thou seen that which backsliding Israel hath done? she is gone up upon every high mountain and under every green tree, and there hath played the harlot. And I said after she had done all these things, Turn thou unto me. But she returned not. And her treacherous sister Judah saw it. And I saw, when for all the causes whereby backsliding Israel committed adultery I had put her away, and given her a bill of divorce; yet her treacherous sister Judah feared not, but went and played the harlot also. And it came to pass through the lightness of her whoredom, that she defiled the land, and committed adultery with stones and with stocks. And yet for all this her treacherous sister Judah hath not turned unto me with her whole heart, but feignedly, saith the Lord.

And the Lord said unto me, The backsliding Israel hath justified herself more than treacherous Judah. Go and proclaim these words toward the north, and say, Return, thou backsliding Israel, saith the Lord; and I will not cause mine anger to fall upon you: for I am merciful, saith the Lord, and I will not keep anger for ever. Only acknowledge thine iniquity, that thou hast transgressed against the Lord thy God, and hast scattered thy ways to the strangers under every green tree, and ye have not obeyed my voice, saith the Lord.

Turn, O backsliding children, saith the Lord; for I am married unto you: and I will take you one of a city, and two of a family, and I will bring you to Zion: And I will give you pastors according to mine heart, which shall feed you with knowledge and understanding. And it shall come to pass, when ye be multiplied and increased in the land, in those days, saith the Lord, they shall say no more, The ark of the covenant of the Lord: neither shall it come to mind: neither shall they remember it; neither shall they visit it; neither shall that be done any more. At that time they shall call Jerusalem the throne of the Lord; and all the nations shall be gathered unto it, to the name of the Lord, to Jerusalem: neither shall they walk any more after the imagination of their evil heart.

GOD'S JUDGMENT ON HIS PEOPLE
Jeremiah 4:23 – 5:3, 26–31, 6:13–20

I beheld the earth, and, lo, it was without form, and void;
    and the heavens, and they had no light.
I beheld the mountains, and, lo, they trembled,
    and all the hills moved lightly.
I beheld, and, lo, there was no man,
    and all the birds of the heavens were fled.
I beheld, and, lo, the fruitful place was a wilderness,
    and all the cities thereof were broken down
    at the presence of the Lord, and by his fierce anger.

For thus hath the Lord said,

The whole land shall be desolate;
    yet will I not make a full end.
For this shall the earth mourn, and the heavens above be black:
    because I have spoken it, I have purposed it,
    and will not repent, neither will I turn back from it.

The whole city shall flee
  for the noise of the horsemen and bowmen;
they shall go into thickets, and climb up upon the rocks:
  every city shall be forsaken, and not a man dwell therein.
And when thou art spoiled, what wilt thou do?
Though thou clothest thyself with crimson,
  though thou deckest thee with ornaments of gold,
  though thou rentest thy face with painting,
in vain shalt thou make thyself fair;
  thy lovers will despise thee, they will seek thy life.

For I have heard a voice as of a woman in travail,
  and the anguish as of her that bringeth forth her first child,
the voice of the daughter of Zion, that bewaileth herself,
  that spreadeth her hands, saying,
Woe is me now! for my soul is wearied because of murderers.

Run ye to and fro through the streets of Jerusalem,
  and see now, and know,
and seek in the broad places thereof,
  if ye can find a man,
if there be any that executeth judgment,
  that seeketh the truth; and I will pardon it.
And though they say, The Lord liveth;
  surely they swear falsely.

O Lord, are not thine eyes upon the truth?
Thou hast stricken them,
  but they have not grieved;
thou hast consumed them,
  but they have refused to receive correction:
they have made their faces harder than a rock;
  they have refused to return...

For among my people are found wicked men:
  they lay wait, as he that setteth snares;
  they set a trap, they catch men.
As a cage is full of birds, so are their houses full of deceit:
  therefore they are become great, and waxen rich.

They are waxen fat, they shine:
> yea, they overpass the deeds of the wicked:
> they judge not the cause, the cause of the fatherless,
yet they prosper;
> and the right of the needy do they not judge.
Shall I not visit for these things?
>> saith the Lord:
> shall not my soul be avenged on such a nation as this?

A wonderful and horrible thing is committed in the land;
The prophets prophesy falsely,
> and the priests bear rule by their means;
and my people love to have it so:
> and what will ye do in the end thereof?...

For from the least of them even unto the greatest of them
> every one is given to covetousness;
and from the prophet even unto the priest
> every one dealeth falsely.
They have healed also the hurt
> of the daughter of my people slightly, saying,
> Peace, peace; when there is no peace.
Were they ashamed when they had committed abomination?
> nay, they were not at all ashamed,
> neither could they blush:
therefore they shall fall among them that fall:
> at the time that I visit them they shall be cast down,
>> saith the Lord.

Thus saith the Lord,

Stand ye in the ways, and see, and ask for the old paths,
> where is the good way, and walk therein,
> and ye shall find rest for your souls.
But they said, We will not walk therein.
Also I set watchmen over you, saying,
> Hearken to the sound of the trumpet.
But they said,
> We will not hearken.

Therefore hear, ye nations, and know, O congregation,
    what is among them.
Hear, O earth: behold, I will bring evil upon this people,
    even the fruit of their thoughts,
because they have not hearkened unto my words,
    nor to my law, but rejected it.
To what purpose cometh there to me incense from Sheba,
    and the sweet cane from a far country?
Your burnt offerings are not acceptable,
    nor your sacrifices sweet unto me.

TRUE WORSHIP
Jeremiah 7:1–11, 25–29

The word that came to Jeremiah from the Lord, saying, Stand in the gate of the Lord's house, and proclaim there this word, and say, Hear the word of the Lord, all ye of Judah, that enter in at these gates to worship the Lord.

Thus saith the Lord of hosts, the God of Israel, Amend your ways and your doings, and I will cause you to dwell in this place. Trust ye not in lying words, saying, The temple of the Lord, The temple of the Lord, The temple of the Lord, are these. For if ye throughly amend your ways and your doings; if ye throughly execute judgment between a man and his neighbour; if ye oppress not the stranger, the fatherless, and the widow, and shed not innocent blood in this place, neither walk after other gods to your hurt: then will I cause you to dwell in this place, in the land that I gave to your fathers, for ever and ever. Behold, ye trust in lying words, that cannot profit.

Will ye steal, murder, and commit adultery, and swear falsely, and burn incense unto Baal, and walk after other gods whom ye know not; and come and stand before me in this house, which is called by my name, and say, We are delivered to do all these abominations? Is this house, which is called by my name, become a den of robbers in your eyes? Behold, even I have seen it, saith the Lord...

Since the day that your fathers came forth out of the land of Egypt unto this day I have even sent unto you all my servants the prophets, daily rising up early and sending them: yet they hearkened not unto me, nor inclined their ear, but hardened their neck: they did worse than their fathers.

Therefore thou shalt speak all these words unto them; but they will not hearken to thee: thou shalt also call unto them; but they will not answer thee. But thou shalt say unto them, This is a nation that obeyeth not the voice of the Lord their God, nor receiveth correction: truth is perished, and is cut off from their mouth. Cut off thine hair, O Jerusalem, and cast it away, and take up a lamentation on high places; for the Lord hath rejected and forsaken the generation of his wrath.

TRUE WISDOM
Jeremiah 8:4–12, 9:23–24

Moreover thou shalt say unto them, Thus saith the Lord;

Shall they fall, and not arise?
    shall he turn away, and not return?
Why then is this people of Jerusalem slidden back
    by a perpetual backsliding?
    they hold fast deceit, they refuse to return.
I hearkened and heard, but they spake not aright:
    no man repented him of his wickedness, saying,
    What have I done?
every one turned to his course,
    as the horse rusheth into the battle.
Yea, the stork in the heaven knoweth her appointed times;
    and the turtle and the crane and the swallow
    observe the time of their coming;
but my people know not the judgment of the Lord.

How do ye say,
    We are wise, and the law of the Lord is with us?
Lo, certainly in vain made he it;
    the pen of the scribes is in vain.

The wise men are ashamed,
    they are dismayed and taken:
lo, they have rejected the word of the Lord;
    and what wisdom is in them?
Therefore will I give their wives unto others,
    and their fields to them that shall inherit them:
for every one from the least even unto the greatest
    is given to covetousness,
from the prophet even unto the priest
    every one dealeth falsely.
For they have healed
    the hurt of the daughter of my people slightly, saying,
    Peace, peace; when there is no peace.
Were they ashamed when they had committed abomination?
    nay, they were not at all ashamed,
    neither could they blush:
therefore shall they fall among them that fall:
    in the time of their visitation they shall be cast down...

Thus saith the Lord,

Let not the wise man glory in his wisdom,
    neither let the mighty man glory in his might,
    let not the rich man glory in his riches:
But let him that glorieth glory in this,
    that he understandeth and knoweth me,
that I am the Lord which exercise lovingkindness, judgment,
    and righteousness, in the earth: for in these things I delight,
        saith the Lord.

THE LINEN GIRDLE
Jeremiah 13:1–11

Thus saith the Lord unto me, Go and get thee a linen girdle, and put it upon thy loins, and put it not in water. So I got a girdle according to the word of the Lord, and put it on my loins.

And the word of the Lord came unto me the second time, saying,

Take the girdle that thou hast got, which is upon thy loins, and arise, go to Euphrates, and hide it there in a hole of the rock. So I went, and hid it by Euphrates, as the Lord commanded me. And it came to pass after many days, that the Lord said unto me, Arise, go to Euphrates, and take the girdle from thence, which I commanded thee to hide there. Then I went to Euphrates, and digged, and took the girdle from the place where I had hid it: and, behold, the girdle was marred, it was profitable for nothing.

Then the word of the Lord came unto me, saying, Thus saith the Lord, after this manner will I mar the pride of Judah, and the great pride of Jerusalem. This evil people, which refuse to hear my words, which walk in the imagination of their heart, and walk after other gods, to serve them, and to worship them, shall even be as this girdle, which is good for nothing. For as the girdle cleaveth to the loins of a man, so have I caused to cleave unto me the whole house of Israel and the whole house of Judah, saith the Lord; that they might be unto me for a people, and for a name, and for a praise, and for a glory: but they would not hear.

JERUSALEM'S SHAME
Jeremiah 13:23–27

Can the Ethiopian change his skin, or the leopard his spots?
    then may ye also do good, that are accustomed to do evil.
Therefore will I scatter them as the stubble that passeth away
    by the wind of the wilderness.
This is thy lot, the portion of thy measures from me,
      saith the Lord;
    because thou hast forgotten me, and trusted in falsehood.
Therefore will I discover thy skirts upon thy face,
    that thy shame may appear.
I have seen thine adulteries, and thy neighings,
    the lewdness of thy whoredom,
    and thine abominations on the hills in the fields.
Woe unto thee, O Jerusalem! wilt thou not be made clean?
    when shall it once be?

JEREMIAH'S COMPLAINT
Jeremiah 15:10–21

Woe is me, my mother,
    that thou hast borne me a man of strife
    and a man of contention to the whole earth!
I have neither lent on usury,
    nor men have lent to me on usury;
    yet every one of them doth curse me.

The Lord said,

Verily it shall be well with thy remnant;
    verily I will cause the enemy to entreat thee well
    in the time of evil and in the time of affliction.
Shall iron break the northern iron and the steel?
Thy substance and thy treasures
    will I give to the spoil without price,
    and that for all thy sins, even in all thy borders.
And I will make thee to pass with thine enemies
    into a land which thou knowest not:
for a fire is kindled in mine anger, which shall burn upon you.

O Lord, thou knowest: remember me, and visit me,
    and revenge me of my persecutors;
take me not away in thy longsuffering:
    know that for thy sake I have suffered rebuke.
Thy words were found, and I did eat them;
    and thy word was unto me the joy and rejoicing of mine heart:
    for I am called by thy name, O Lord God of hosts.
I sat not in the assembly of the mockers,
    nor rejoiced;
I sat alone because of thy hand:
    for thou hast filled me with indignation.
Why is my pain perpetual, and my wound incurable,
    which refuseth to be healed?
wilt thou be altogether unto me as a liar,
    and as waters that fail?

Therefore thus saith the Lord,

If thou return, then will I bring thee again,
  and thou shalt stand before me:
and if thou take forth the precious from the vile,
  thou shalt be as my mouth:
let them return unto thee;
  but return not thou unto them.
And I will make thee unto this people a fenced brasen wall:
  and they shall fight against thee,
but they shall not prevail against thee:
    for I am with thee to save thee and to deliver thee,
      saith the Lord.
And I will deliver thee out of the hand of the wicked,
  and I will redeem thee out of the hand of the terrible.

SOME WISE SAYINGS
Jeremiah 17:5–11

Thus saith the Lord;

Cursed be the man that trusteth in man,
  and maketh flesh his arm,
  and whose heart departeth from the Lord.
For he shall be like the heath in the desert,
  and shall not see when good cometh;
but shall inhabit the parched places in the wilderness,
  in a salt land and not inhabited.

Blessed is the man that trusteth in the Lord,
  and whose hope the Lord is.
For he shall be as a tree planted by the waters,
  and that spreadeth out her roots by the river,
and shall not see when heat cometh,
  but her leaf shall be green;
and shall not be careful in the year of drought,
  neither shall cease from yielding fruit.

The heart is deceitful above all things,
    and desperately wicked: who can know it?
I the Lord search the heart,
I try the reins, even to give every man according to his ways,
    and according to the fruit of his doings.

As the partridge sitteth on eggs, and hatcheth them not;
    so he that getteth riches, and not by right,
shall leave them in the midst of his days,
    and at his end shall be a fool.

A PRAYER FOR VENGEANCE
Jeremiah 17:14–18

Heal me, O Lord, and I shall be healed;
    save me, and I shall be saved: for thou art my praise.
Behold, they say unto me,
    Where is the word of the Lord? let it come now.
As for me, I have not hastened from being a pastor to follow thee:
    neither have I desired the woeful day;
thou knowest: that which came out of my lips
    was right before thee.
Be not a terror unto me:
    thou art my hope in the day of evil.
Let them be confounded that persecute me,
    but let not me be confounded:
let them be dismayed,
    but let not me be dismayed:
bring upon them the day of evil,
    and destroy them with double destruction.

THE POTTER AND THE CLAY
Jeremiah 18:1–12

The word which came to Jeremiah from the Lord, saying, Arise, and
go down to the potter's house, and there I will cause thee to hear my

words. Then I went down to the potter's house, and, behold, he wrought a work on the wheels. And the vessel that he made of clay was marred in the hand of the potter: so he made it again another vessel, as seemed good to the potter to make it.

Then the word of the Lord came to me, saying, O house of Israel, cannot I do with you as this potter? saith the Lord. Behold, as the clay is in the potter's hand, so are ye in mine hand, O house of Israel. At what instant I shall speak concerning a nation, and concerning a kingdom, to pluck up, and to pull down, and to destroy it; if that nation, against whom I have pronounced, turn from their evil, I will repent of the evil that I thought to do unto them. And at what instant I shall speak concerning a nation, and concerning a kingdom, to build and to plant it; if it do evil in my sight, that it obey not my voice, then I will repent of the good, wherewith I said I would benefit them.

Now therefore go to, speak to the men of Judah, and to the inhabitants of Jerusalem, saying, Thus saith the Lord; Behold, I frame evil against you, and devise a device against you: return ye now every one from his evil way, and make your ways and your doings good. And they said, There is no hope: but we will walk after our own devices, and we will every one do the imagination of his evil heart.

THE BROKEN BOTTLE
Jeremiah 19:1–3, 10–13

Thus saith the Lord, Go and get a potter's earthen bottle, and take of the ancients of the people, and of the ancients of the priests; and go forth unto the valley of the son of Hinnom, which is by the entry of the east gate, and proclaim there the words that I shall tell thee, and say, Hear ye the word of the Lord, O kings of Judah, and inhabitants of Jerusalem; Thus saith the Lord of hosts, the God of Israel; Behold, I will bring evil upon this place, the which whosoever heareth, his ears shall tingle...

Then shalt thou break the bottle in the sight of the men that go with thee, and shalt say unto them, Thus saith the Lord of hosts; Even so will I break this people and this city, as one breaketh a potter's vessel, that cannot be made whole again: and they shall bury them in

Tophet, till there be no place to bury. Thus will I do unto this place, saith the Lord, and to the inhabitants thereof, and even make this city as Tophet: and the houses of Jerusalem, and the houses of the kings of Judah, shall be defiled as the place of Tophet, because of all the houses upon whose roofs they have burned incense unto all the host of heaven, and have poured out drink offerings unto other gods.

JEREMIAH'S CONFESSIONS
Jeremiah 20:7–18

O Lord, thou hast deceived me, and I was deceived:
  thou art stronger than I, and hast prevailed:
I am in derision daily,
  every one mocketh me.
For since I spake, I cried out, I cried violence and spoil;
  because the word of the Lord was made a reproach unto me,
  and a derision, daily.
Then I said, I will not make mention of him,
  nor speak any more in his name.
But his word was in mine heart
  as a burning fire shut up in my bones,
and I was weary with forbearing,
  and I could not stay.
For I heard the defaming of many,
  fear on every side.
Report, say they, and we will report it.
All my familiars watched for my halting, saying,
Peradventure he will be enticed,
  and we shall prevail against him,
  and we shall take our revenge on him.

But the Lord is with me as a mighty terrible one:
  therefore my persecutors shall stumble,
  and they shall not prevail:
they shall be greatly ashamed; for they shall not prosper:
  their everlasting confusion shall never be forgotten.

But, O Lord of hosts, that triest the righteous,
    and seest the reins and the heart,
let me see thy vengeance on them:
    for unto thee have I opened my cause.

Sing unto the Lord, praise ye the Lord:
    for he hath delivered the soul of the poor
    from the hand of evildoers.

Cursed be the day wherein I was born:
    let not the day wherein my mother bare me be blessed.
Cursed be the man who brought tidings to my father, saying,
    A man child is born unto thee; making him very glad.
And let that man be as the cities which the Lord overthrew,
    and repented not:
and let him hear the cry in the morning,
    and the shouting at noontide;
Because he slew me not from the womb;
    or that my mother might have been my grave,
    and her womb to be always great with me.
Wherefore came I forth out of the womb
    to see labour and sorrow,
    that my days should be consumed with shame?

THE RIGHTEOUS BRANCH
Jeremiah 23:1–8

Woe be unto the pastors that destroy and scatter the sheep of my pasture! saith the Lord. Therefore thus saith the Lord God of Israel against the pastors that feed my people; Ye have scattered my flock, and driven them away, and have not visited them: behold, I will visit upon you the evil of your doings, saith the Lord. And I will gather the remnant of my flock out of all countries whither I have driven them, and will bring them again to their folds; and they shall be fruitful and increase. And I will set up shepherds over them which shall feed them: and they shall fear no more, nor be dismayed, neither shall they be lacking, saith the Lord.

Behold, the days come,
    saith the Lord,
  that I will raise unto David a righteous Branch,
and a King shall reign and prosper,
    and shall execute judgment and justice in the earth.
In his days Judah shall be saved,
    and Israel shall dwell safely:
and this is his name whereby he shall be called,
    The Lord our Righteousness.

Therefore, behold, the days come, saith the Lord, that they shall no more say, The Lord liveth, which brought up the children of Israel out of the land of Egypt; But, The Lord liveth, which brought up and which led the seed of the house of Israel out of the north country, and from all countries whither I had driven them; and they shall dwell in their own land.

THE BASKETS OF FIGS
Jeremiah 24

The Lord shewed me, and, behold, two baskets of figs were set before the temple of the Lord, after that Nebuchadrezzar king of Babylon had carried away captive Jeconiah the son of Jehoiakim king of Judah, and the princes of Judah, with the carpenters and smiths, from Jerusalem, and had brought them to Babylon. One basket had very good figs, even like the figs that are first ripe: and the other basket had very naughty figs, which could not be eaten, they were so bad.

Then said the Lord unto me, What seest thou, Jeremiah? And I said, Figs; the good figs, very good; and the evil, very evil, that cannot be eaten, they are so evil.

Again the word of the Lord came unto me, saying, Thus saith the Lord, the God of Israel; Like these good figs, so will I acknowledge them that are carried away captive of Judah, whom I have sent out of this place into the land of the Chaldeans for their good. For I will set mine eyes upon them for good, and I will bring them again to this land: and I will build them, and not pull them down; and I will plant them, and not pluck them up. And I will give them an heart to know me, that I am the Lord: and they shall be my people, and I will be their God: for they shall return unto me with their whole heart.

And as the evil figs, which cannot be eaten, they are so evil; surely thus saith the Lord, So will I give Zedekiah the king of Judah, and his princes, and the residue of Jerusalem, that remain in this land, and them that dwell in the land of Egypt: And I will deliver them to be removed into all the kingdoms of the earth for their hurt, to be a reproach and a proverb, a taunt and a curse, in all places whither I shall drive them. And I will send the sword, the famine, and the pestilence, among them, till they be consumed from off the land that I gave unto them and to their fathers.

JEREMIAH'S LETTER TO THE EXILES
Jeremiah 29:1, 4–14

Now these are the words of the letter that Jeremiah the prophet sent from Jerusalem unto the residue of the elders which were carried away captives, and to the priests, and to the prophets, and to all the people whom Nebuchadnezzar had carried away captive from Jerusalem to Babylon...

Thus saith the Lord of hosts, the God of Israel, unto all that are carried away captives, whom I have caused to be carried away from Jerusalem unto Babylon; Build ye houses, and dwell in them; and plant gardens, and eat the fruit of them; take ye wives, and beget sons and daughters; and take wives for your sons, and give your daughters to husbands, that they may bear sons and daughters; that ye may be increased there, and not diminished. And seek the peace of the city whither I have caused you to be carried away captives, and pray unto the Lord for it: for in the peace thereof shall ye have peace. For thus saith the Lord of hosts, the God of Israel; Let not your prophets and your diviners, that be in the midst of you, deceive you, neither hearken to your dreams which ye cause to be dreamed. For they prophesy falsely unto you in my name: I have not sent them, saith the Lord.

For thus saith the Lord, That after seventy years be accomplished at Babylon I will visit you, and perform my good word toward you, in causing you to return to this place. For I know the thoughts that I think toward you, saith the Lord, thoughts of peace, and not of evil, to give you an expected end. Then shall ye call upon me, and ye shall go and pray unto me, and I will hearken unto you. And ye shall seek me, and find me, when ye shall search for me with all your heart. And I will be found of you, saith the Lord: and I will turn away your captivity, and I will gather you from all the nations, and from all the places whither I have driven you, saith the Lord; and I will bring you again into the place whence I caused you to be carried away captive.

A PROPHECY OF CONSOLATION
Jeremiah 31:1–17

At the same time, saith the Lord, will I be the God of all the families of Israel, and they shall be my people. Thus saith the Lord,

The people which were left of the sword
    found grace in the wilderness;
even Israel, when I went to cause him to rest.

The Lord hath appeared of old unto me, saying,

Yea, I have loved thee with an everlasting love:
    therefore with lovingkindness have I drawn thee.
Again I will build thee, and thou shalt be built,
    O virgin of Israel:
thou shalt again be adorned with thy tabrets,
    and shalt go forth in the dances of them that make merry.
Thou shalt yet plant vines upon the mountains of Samaria:
    the planters shall plant, and shall eat them as common things.
For there shall be a day,
    that the watchmen upon the mount Ephraim shall cry,
Arise ye, and let us go up to Zion unto the Lord our God.

For thus saith the Lord;

Sing with gladness for Jacob,
and shout among the chief of the nations:
publish ye, praise ye, and say,
O Lord, save thy people, the remnant of Israel.
Behold, I will bring them from the north country,
and gather them from the coasts of the earth,
and with them the blind and the lame, the woman with child
and her that travaileth with child together:
a great company shall return thither.
They shall come with weeping,
and with supplications will I lead them:
I will cause them to walk by the rivers of waters in a straight way,
wherein they shall not stumble:
for I am a father to Israel, and Ephraim is my firstborn.

Hear the word of the Lord, O ye nations,
and declare it in the isles afar off, and say,
He that scattered Israel will gather him, and keep him,
as a shepherd doth his flock.
For the Lord hath redeemed Jacob,
and ransomed him
from the hand of him that was stronger than he.
Therefore they shall come and sing in the height of Zion,
and shall flow together to the goodness of the Lord,
for wheat, and for wine, and for oil,
and for the young of the flock and of the herd:
and their soul shall be as a watered garden;
and they shall not sorrow any more at all.
Then shall the virgin rejoice in the dance,
both young men and old together:
for I will turn their mourning into joy,
and will comfort them,
and make them rejoice from their sorrow.
And I will satiate the soul of the priests with fatness,
and my people shall be satisfied with my goodness,
saith the Lord.

Thus saith the Lord;

> A voice was heard in Ramah,
>   lamentation, and bitter weeping;
> Rachel weeping for her children
>   refused to be comforted for her children,
>   because they were not.

Thus saith the Lord; Refrain thy voice from weeping, and thine eyes from tears: for thy work shall be rewarded, saith the Lord; and they shall come again from the land of the enemy. And there is hope in thine end, saith the Lord, that thy children shall come again to their own border.

THE NEW COVENANT
Jeremiah 31:31–34

Behold, the days come, saith the Lord, that I will make a new covenant with the house of Israel, and with the house of Judah: Not according to the covenant that I made with their fathers in the day that I took them by the hand to bring them out of the land of Egypt; which my covenant they brake, although I was an husband unto them, saith the Lord: But this shall be the covenant that I will make with the house of Israel; After those days, saith the Lord, I will put my law in their inward parts, and write it in their hearts; and will be their God, and they shall be my people. And they shall teach no more every man his neighbour, and every man his brother, saying, Know the Lord: for they shall all know me, from the least of them unto the greatest of them, saith the Lord: for I will forgive their iniquity, and I will remember their sin no more.

PROPHETS
DURING THE EXILE

Ezekiel

Lamentations

Obadiah

Second Isaiah

Ezekiel

THE VISION OF THE HEAVENLY CHARIOT
Ezekiel 1

Now it came to pass in the thirtieth year, in the fourth month, in the fifth day of the month, as I was among the captives by the river of Chebar, that the heavens were opened, and I saw visions of God.

In the fifth day of the month, which was the fifth year of king Jehoiachin's captivity, the word of the Lord came expressly unto Ezekiel the priest, the son of Buzi, in the land of the Chaldeans by the river Chebar; and the hand of the Lord was there upon him.

And I looked, and, behold, a whirlwind came out of the north, a great cloud, and a fire infolding itself, and a brightness was about it, and out of the midst thereof as the colour of amber, out of the midst of the fire. Also out of the midst thereof came the likeness of four living creatures. And this was their appearance; they had the likeness of a man. And every one had four faces, and every one had four wings. And their feet were straight feet; and the sole of their feet was like the sole of a calf's foot: and they sparkled like the colour of burnished brass. And they had the hands of a man under their wings on their four sides; and they four had their faces and their wings. Their wings were joined one to another; they turned not when they went; they went every one straight forward.

As for the likeness of their faces, they four had the face of a man, and the face of a lion, on the right side: and they four had the face of an ox on the left side; they four also had the face of an eagle. Thus were their faces: and their wings were stretched upward; two wings of every one were joined one to another, and two covered their bodies. And they went every one straight forward: whither the spirit was to go, they went; and they turned not when they went. As for the likeness of the living creatures, their appearance was like burning coals of fire, and like the appearance of lamps: it went up and down among the living creatures; and the fire was bright, and out of the fire went forth lightning. And the living creatures ran and returned as the appearance of a flash of lightning.

Now as I beheld the living creatures, behold one wheel upon the earth by the living creatures, with his four faces. The appearance of the wheels and their work was like unto the colour of a beryl: and they four had one likeness: and their appearance and their work was as it were a wheel in the middle of a wheel. When they went, they went upon their four sides: and they turned not when they went. As for their rings, they were so high that they were dreadful; and their rings were full of eyes round about them four. And when the living creatures went, the wheels went by them: and when the living creatures were lifted up from the earth, the wheels were lifted up. Whithersoever the spirit was to go, they went, thither was their spirit to go; and the wheels were lifted up over against them: for the spirit of the living creature was in the wheels. When those went, these went; and when those stood, these stood; and when those were lifted up from the earth, the wheels were lifted up over against them: for the spirit of the living creature was in the wheels.

And the likeness of the firmament upon the heads of the living creature was as the colour of the terrible crystal, stretched forth over their heads above. And under the firmament were their wings straight, the one toward the other: every one had two, which covered on this side, and every one had two, which covered on that side, their bodies. And when they went, I heard the noise of their wings, like the noise of great waters, as the voice of the Almighty, the voice of speech, as the noise of an host: when they stood, they let down their wings.

And there was a voice from the firmament that was over their heads, when they stood, and had let down their wings. And above the firmament that was over their heads was the likeness of a throne, as the appearance of a sapphire stone: and upon the likeness of the throne was the likeness as the appearance of a man above upon it. And I saw as the colour of amber, as the appearance of fire round about within it, from the appearance of his loins even upward, and from the appearance of his loins even downward, I saw as it were the appearance of fire, and it had brightness round about.

As the appearance of the bow that is in the cloud in the day of rain, so was the appearance of the brightness round about. This was the appearance of the likeness of the glory of the Lord. And when I saw it, I fell upon my face, and I heard a voice of one that spake.

THE CALL OF EZEKIEL
Ezekiel 2:1–4, 8–10; 3:1–3, 10–14

And he said unto me, Son of man, stand upon thy feet, and I will speak unto thee. And the spirit entered into me when he spake unto me, and set me upon my feet, that I heard him that spake unto me.

And he said unto me, Son of man, I send thee to the children of Israel, to a rebellious nation that hath rebelled against me: they and their fathers have transgressed against me, even unto this very day. For they are impudent children and stiffhearted. I do send thee unto them; and thou shalt say unto them, Thus saith the Lord God... But thou, son of man, hear what I say unto thee; Be not thou rebellious like that rebellious house: open thy mouth, and eat that I give thee.

And when I looked, behold, an hand was sent unto me; and, lo, a roll of a book was therein; And he spread it before me; and it was written within and without: and there was written therein lamentations, and mourning, and woe. Moreover he said unto me, Son of man, eat that thou findest; eat this roll, and go speak unto the house of Israel.

So I opened my mouth, and he caused me to eat that roll. And he said unto me, Son of man, cause thy belly to eat, and fill thy bowels with this roll that I give thee. Then did I eat it; and it was in my mouth as honey for sweetness... Moreover he said unto me, Son of man, all my words that I shall speak unto thee receive in thine heart, and hear with thine ears. And go, get thee to them of the captivity, unto the children of thy people, and speak unto them, and tell them, Thus saith the Lord God; whether they will hear, or whether they will forbear.

Then the spirit took me up, and I heard behind me a voice of a great rushing, saying, Blessed be the glory of the Lord from his place. I heard also the noise of the wings of the living creatures that touched one another, and the noise of the wheels over against them, and a noise of a great rushing. So the spirit lifted me up, and took me away, and I went in bitterness, in the heat of my spirit; but the hand of the Lord was strong upon me.

GOD'S WATCHMAN
Ezekiel 3:15–21

Then I came to them of the captivity at Telabib, that dwelt by the river of Chebar, and I sat where they sat, and remained there astonished among them seven days. And it came to pass at the end of seven days, that the word of the Lord came unto me, saying, Son of man, I have made thee a watchman unto the house of Israel: therefore hear the word at my mouth, and give them warning from me. When I say unto the wicked, Thou shalt surely die; and thou givest him not warning, nor speakest to warn the wicked from his wicked way, to save his life; the same wicked man shall die in his iniquity; but his blood will I require at thine hand. Yet if thou warn the wicked, and he turn not from his wickedness, nor from his wicked way, he shall die in his iniquity; but thou hast delivered thy soul.

Again, when a righteous man doth turn from his righteousness, and commit iniquity, and I lay a stumblingblock before him, he shall die: because thou hast not given him warning, he shall die in his sin, and his righteousness which he hath done shall not be remembered; but his blood will I require at thine hand. Nevertheless if thou warn the righteous man, that the righteous sin not, and he doth not sin, he shall surely live, because he is warned; also thou hast delivered thy soul.

EZEKIEL IS STRUCK DUMB
Ezekiel 3:22–27

And the hand of the Lord was there upon me; and he said unto me, Arise, go forth into the plain, and I will there talk with thee. Then I arose, and went forth into the plain: and, behold, the glory of the Lord stood there, as the glory which I saw by the river of Chebar: and I fell on my face.

Then the spirit entered into me, and set me upon my feet, and spake with me, and said unto me, Go, shut thyself within thine house. But thou, O son of man, behold, they shall put bands upon thee, and shall bind thee with them, and thou shalt not go out among them: and I will make thy tongue cleave to the roof of thy mouth, that thou shalt be dumb, and shalt not be to them a reprover: for they are a rebellious house. But when I speak with thee, I will open thy mouth, and thou shalt say unto them, Thus saith the Lord God; He that heareth, let him hear; and he that forbeareth, let him forbear: for they are a rebellious house.

THE SIEGE OF JERUSALEM FORETOLD
Ezekiel 4:1-11

Thou also, son of man, take thee a tile, and lay it before thee, and pourtray upon it the city, even Jerusalem: and lay siege against it, and build a fort against it, and cast a mount against it; set the camp also against it, and set battering rams against it round about. Moreover take thou unto thee an iron pan, and set it for a wall of iron between thee and the city: and set thy face against it, and it shall be besieged, and thou shalt lay siege against it. This shall be a sign to the house of Israel.

Lie thou also upon thy left side, and lay the iniquity of the house of Israel upon it: according to the number of the days that thou shalt lie upon it thou shalt bear their iniquity. For I have laid upon thee the years of their iniquity, according to the number of the days, three hundred and ninety days: so shalt thou bear the iniquity of the house of Israel.

And when thou hast accomplished them, lie again on thy right side, and thou shalt bear the iniquity of the house of Judah forty days: I have appointed thee each day for a year.

Therefore thou shalt set thy face toward the siege of Jerusalem, and thine arm shall be uncovered, and thou shalt prophesy against it. And, behold, I will lay bands upon thee, and thou shalt not turn thee from one side to another, till thou hast ended the days of thy siege.

Take thou also unto thee wheat, and barley, and beans, and lentiles, and millet, and fitches, and put them in one vessel, and make thee bread thereof, according to the number of the days that thou shalt lie upon thy side, three hundred and ninety days shalt thou eat thereof. And thy meat which thou shalt eat shall be by weight, twenty shekels a day: from time to time shalt thou eat it. Thou shalt drink also water by measure, the sixth part of an hin: from time to time shalt thou drink.

ISRAEL'S IDOLATRY
Ezekiel 8

And it came to pass in the sixth year, in the sixth month, in the fifth day of the month, as I sat in mine house, and the elders of Judah sat before me, that the hand of the Lord God fell there upon me. Then I beheld, and lo a likeness as the appearance of fire: from the appearance of his loins even downward, fire; and from his loins even upward, as the appearance of brightness, as the colour of amber. And he put forth the form of an hand, and took me by a lock of mine head; and the spirit lifted me up between the earth and the heaven, and brought me in the visions of God to Jerusalem, to the door of the inner gate that looketh toward the north; where was the seat of the image of jealousy, which provoketh to jealousy. And, behold, the glory of the God of Israel was there, according to the vision that I saw in the plain.

Then said he unto me, Son of man, lift up thine eyes now the way toward the north. So I lifted up mine eyes the way toward the north, and behold northward at the gate of the altar this image of jealousy in the entry.

He said furthermore unto me, Son of man, seest thou what they do? even the great abominations that the house of Israel committeth here, that I should go far off from my sanctuary? but turn thee yet again, and thou shalt see greater abominations. And he brought me to the door of the court; and when I looked, behold a hole in the wall.

Then said he unto me, Son of man, dig now in the wall: and when I had digged in the wall, behold a door. And he said unto me, Go in, and behold the wicked abominations that they do here. So I went in and saw; and behold every form of creeping things, and abominable beasts, and all the idols of the house of Israel, pourtrayed upon the wall round about. And there stood before them several men of the ancients of the house of Israel, and in the midst of them stood Jaazaniah the son of Shaphan, with every man his censer in his hand; and a thick cloud of incense went up.

Then said he unto me, Son of man, hast thou seen what the ancients of the house of Israel do in the dark, every man in the chambers of his imagery? for they say, The Lord seeth us not; the Lord hath forsaken the earth. He said also unto me, Turn thee yet again, and thou shalt see greater abominations that they do.

Then he brought me to the door of the gate of the Lord's house which was toward the north; and, behold, there sat women weeping for Tammuz. Then said he unto me, Hast thou seen this, O son of man? turn thee yet again, and thou shalt see greater abominations than these.

And he brought me into the inner court of the Lord's house, and, behold, at the door of the temple of the Lord, between the porch and the altar, were about five and twenty men, with their backs toward the temple of the Lord, and their faces toward the east; and they worshipped the sun toward the east.

Then he said unto me, Hast thou seen this, O son of man? Is it a light thing to the house of Judah that they commit the abominations which they commit here? for they have filled the land with violence, and have returned to provoke me to anger: and, lo, they put the branch to their nose. Therefore will I also deal in fury: mine eye shall not spare, neither will I have pity: and though they cry in mine ears with a loud voice, yet will I not hear them.

GOD'S PUNISHMENT ON JERUSALEM
Ezekiel 9

He cried also in mine ears with a loud voice, saying, Cause them that have charge over the city to draw near, even every man with his destroying weapon in his hand. And, behold, six men came from the way of the higher gate, which lieth toward the north, and every man a slaughter weapon in his hand; and one man among them was clothed with linen, with a writer's inkhorn by his side: and they went in, and stood beside the brasen altar.

And the glory of the God of Israel was gone up from the cherub, whereupon he was, to the threshold of the house. And he called to the man clothed with linen, which had the writer's inkhorn by his side; and the Lord said unto him, Go through the midst of the city, through the midst of Jerusalem, and set a mark upon the foreheads of the men that sigh and that cry for all the abominations that be done in the midst thereof.

And to the others he said in mine hearing, Go ye after him through the city, and smite: let not your eye spare, neither have ye pity: slay utterly old and young, both maids, and little children, and women: but come not near any man upon whom is the mark; and begin at my sanctuary. Then they began at the ancient men which were before the house.

And he said unto them, Defile the house, and fill the courts with the slain: go ye forth. And they went forth, and slew in the city. And it came to pass, while they were slaying them, and I was left, that I fell upon my face, and cried, and said, Ah Lord God! wilt thou destroy all the residue of Israel in thy pouring out of thy fury upon Jerusalem?

Then said he unto me, The iniquity of the house of Israel and Judah is exceeding great, and the land is full of blood, and the city full of perverseness: for they say, The Lord hath forsaken the earth, and the Lord seeth not. And as for me also, mine eye shall not spare, neither will I have pity, but I will recompense their way upon their head.

And, behold, the man clothed with linen, which had the inkhorn by his side, reported the matter, saying, I have done as thou hast commanded me.

THE GLORY OF GOD LEAVES THE TEMPLE
Ezekiel 10:1–7, 18–19, 11:23–25

Then I looked, and, behold, in the firmament that was above the head of the cherubims there appeared over them as it were a sapphire stone, as the appearance of the likeness of a throne. And he spake unto the man clothed with linen, and said, Go in between the wheels, even under the cherub, and fill thine hand with coals of fire from between the cherubims, and scatter them over the city. And he went in in my sight.

Now the cherubims stood on the right side of the house, when the man went in; and the cloud filled the inner court. Then the glory of the Lord went up from the cherub, and stood over the threshold of the house; and the house was filled with the cloud, and the court was full of the brightness of the Lord's glory. And the sound of the cherubims' wings was heard even to the outer court, as the voice of the Almighty God when he speaketh.

And it came to pass, that when he had commanded the man clothed with linen, saying, Take fire from between the wheels, from between the cherubims; then he went in, and stood beside the wheels. And one cherub stretched forth his hand from between the cherubims unto the fire that was between the cherubims, and took thereof, and put it into the hands of him that was clothed with linen: who took it, and went out…

Then the glory of the Lord departed from off the threshold of the house, and stood over the cherubims. And the cherubims lifted up their wings, and mounted up from the earth in my sight: when they went out, the wheels also were beside them, and every one stood at the door of the east gate of the Lord's house; and the glory of the God of Israel was over them above…

And the glory of the Lord went up from the midst of the city, and stood upon the mountain which is on the east side of the city. Afterwards the spirit took me up, and brought me in a vision by the Spirit of God into Chaldea, to them of the captivity.

So the vision that I had seen went up from me. Then I spake unto them of the captivity all the things that the Lord had shewed me.

GOD AND THE SOUL
Ezekiel 18:1–4, 21–24, 29–32

The word of the Lord came unto me again, saying, What mean ye, that ye use this proverb concerning the land of Israel, saying,

The fathers have eaten sour grapes,
and the children's teeth are set on edge?

As I live, saith the Lord God, ye shall not have occasion any more to use this proverb in Israel. Behold, all souls are mine; as the soul of the father, so also the soul of the son is mine: the soul that sinneth, it shall die... The son shall not bear the iniquity of the father, neither shall the father bear the iniquity of the son: the righteousness of the righteous shall be upon him, and the wickedness of the wicked shall be upon him...

But if the wicked will turn from all his sins that he hath committed, and keep all my statutes, and do that which is lawful and right, he shall surely live, he shall not die. All his transgressions that he hath committed, they shall not be mentioned unto him: in his righteousness that he hath done he shall live. Have I any pleasure at all that the wicked should die? saith the Lord God: and not that he should return from his ways, and live?

But when the righteous turneth away from his righteousness, and committeth iniquity, and doeth according to all the abominations that the wicked man doeth, shall he live? All his righteousness that he hath done shall not be mentioned: in his trespass that he hath trespassed, and in his sin that he hath sinned, in them shall he die...

Yet saith the house of Israel, The way of the Lord is not equal. O house of Israel, are not my ways equal? are not your ways unequal? Therefore I will judge you, O house of Israel, every one according to his ways, saith the Lord God. Repent, and turn yourselves from all your transgressions; so iniquity shall not be your ruin. Cast away from you all your transgressions, whereby ye have transgressed; and make you a new heart and a new spirit: for why will ye die, O house of Israel? For I have no pleasure in the death of him that dieth, saith the Lord God: wherefore turn yourselves, and live ye.

EZEKIEL'S WIFE DIES
Ezekiel 24:15–24

Also the word of the Lord came unto me, saying, Son of man, behold, I take away from thee the desire of thine eyes with a stroke: yet neither shalt thou mourn nor weep, neither shall thy tears run down. Forbear to cry, make no mourning for the dead, bind the tire of thine head upon thee, and put on thy shoes upon thy feet, and cover not thy lips, and eat not the bread of men.

So I spake unto the people in the morning: and at even my wife died; and I did in the morning as I was commanded. And the people said unto me, Wilt thou not tell us what these things are to us, that thou doest so?

Then I answered them, The word of the Lord came unto me, saying, Speak unto the house of Israel, Thus saith the Lord God; Behold, I will profane my sanctuary, the excellency of your strength, the desire of your eyes, and that which your soul pitieth; and your sons and your daughters whom ye have left shall fall by the sword. And ye shall do as I have done: ye shall not cover your lips, nor eat the bread of men. And your tires shall be upon your heads, and your shoes upon your feet: ye shall not mourn nor weep; but ye shall pine away for your iniquities, and mourn one toward another. Thus Ezekiel is unto you a sign: according to all that he hath done shall ye do: and when this cometh, ye shall know that I am the Lord God.

THE WICKED SHEPHERDS
Ezekiel 34:1–12

And the word of the Lord came unto me, saying, Son of man, prophesy against the shepherds of Israel, prophesy, and say unto them, Thus saith the Lord God unto the shepherds; Woe be to the shepherds of Israel that do feed themselves! should not the shepherds feed the flocks? Ye eat the fat, and ye clothe you with the wool, ye kill them that are fed: but ye feed not the flock. The diseased have ye not strengthened, neither have ye healed that which was sick, neither have ye bound up that which was broken, neither have ye brought again that which was driven away, neither have ye sought that which was lost; but with force and with cruelty have ye ruled them. And they were scattered, because there is no shepherd: and they became meat to all the beasts of the field, when they were scattered. My sheep wandered through all the mountains, and upon every high hill: yea, my flock was scattered upon all the face of the earth, and none did search or seek after them.

Therefore, ye shepherds, hear the word of the Lord; As I live, saith the Lord God, surely because my flock became a prey, and my flock became meat to every beast of the field, because there was no shepherd, neither did my shepherds search for my flock, but the shepherds fed themselves, and fed not my flock; therefore, O ye shepherds, hear the word of the Lord; Thus saith the Lord God; Behold, I am against the shepherds; and I will require my flock at their hand, and cause them to cease from feeding the flock; neither shall the shepherds feed themselves any more; for I will deliver my flock from their mouth, that they may not be meat for them.

For thus saith the Lord God; Behold, I, even I, will both search my sheep, and seek them out. As a shepherd seeketh out his flock in the day that he is among his sheep that are scattered; so will I seek out my sheep, and will deliver them out of all places where they have been scattered in the cloudy and dark day.

THE RESTORATION OF ISRAEL FORETOLD
Ezekiel 36:16–28

Moreover the word of the Lord came unto me, saying, Son of man, when the house of Israel dwelt in their own land, they defiled it by their own way and by their doings: their way was before me as the uncleanness of a removed woman. Wherefore I poured my fury upon them for the blood that they had shed upon the land, and for their idols wherewith they had polluted it: And I scattered them among the heathen, and they were dispersed through the countries: according to their way and according to their doings I judged them. And when they entered unto the heathen, whither they went, they profaned my holy name, when they said to them, These are the people of the Lord, and are gone forth out of his land. But I had pity for mine holy name, which the house of Israel had profaned among the heathen, whither they went.

Therefore say unto the house of Israel, Thus saith the Lord God; I do not this for your sakes, O house of Israel, but for mine holy name's sake, which ye have profaned among the heathen, whither ye went. And I will sanctify my great name, which was profaned among the heathen, which ye have profaned in the midst of them; and the heathen shall know that I am the Lord, saith the Lord God, when I shall be sanctified in you before their eyes.

For I will take you from among the heathen, and gather you out of all countries, and will bring you into your own land. Then will I sprinkle clean water upon you, and ye shall be clean: from all your filthiness, and from all your idols, will I cleanse you. A new heart also will I give you, and a new spirit will I put within you: and I will take away the stony heart out of your flesh, and I will give you an heart of flesh. And I will put my spirit within you, and cause you to walk in my statutes, and ye shall keep my judgments, and do them. And ye shall dwell in the land that I gave to your fathers; and ye shall be my people, and I will be your God.

THE VISION OF THE VALLEY OF DRY BONES
Ezekiel 37:1–14

The hand of the Lord was upon me, and carried me out in the spirit of the Lord, and set me down in the midst of the valley which was full of bones, and caused me to pass by them round about: and, behold, there were very many in the open valley; and, lo, they were very dry.

And he said unto me, Son of man, can these bones live? And I answered, O Lord God, thou knowest. Again he said unto me, Prophesy upon these bones, and say unto them, O ye dry bones, hear the word of the Lord. Thus saith the Lord God unto these bones; Behold, I will cause breath to enter into you, and ye shall live: and I will lay sinews upon you, and will bring up flesh upon you, and cover you with skin, and put breath in you, and ye shall live; and ye shall know that I am the Lord.

So I prophesied as I was commanded: and as I prophesied, there was a noise, and behold a shaking, and the bones came together, bone to his bone. And when I beheld, lo, the sinews and the flesh came up upon them, and the skin covered them above: but there was no breath in them.

Then said he unto me, Prophesy unto the wind, prophesy, son of man, and say to the wind, Thus saith the Lord God; Come from the four winds, O breath, and breathe upon these slain, that they may live. So I prophesied as he commanded me, and the breath came into them, and they lived, and stood up upon their feet, an exceeding great army. Then he said unto me, Son of man, these bones are the whole house of Israel: behold, they say, Our bones are dried, and our hope is lost: we are cut off for our parts. Therefore prophesy and say unto them, Thus saith the Lord God; Behold, O my people, I will open your graves, and cause you to come up out of your graves, and bring you into the land of Israel. And ye shall know that I am the Lord, when I have opened your graves, O my people, and brought you up out of your graves, and shall put my spirit in you, and ye shall live, and I shall place you in your own land: then shall ye know that I the Lord have spoken it, and performed it, saith the Lord.

THE VISION OF THE TEMPLE
Ezekiel 40:1–6, 43:2–7, 10–11, 44:1–4, 47:1–6, 12, 48:30–35

In the five and twentieth year of our captivity, in the beginning of the year, in the tenth day of the month, in the fourteenth year after that the city was smitten, in the selfsame day the hand of the Lord was upon me, and brought me thither. In the visions of God brought he me into the land of Israel, and set me upon a very high mountain, by which was as the frame of a city on the south. And he brought me thither, and, behold, there was a man, whose appearance was like the appearance of brass, with a line of flax in his hand, and a measuring reed; and he stood in the gate. And the man said unto me, Son of man, behold with thine eyes, and hear with thine ears, and set thine heart upon all that I shall shew thee; for to the intent that I might shew them unto thee art thou brought hither: declare all that thou seest to the house of Israel. And behold a wall on the outside of the house round about, and in the man's hand a measuring reed of six cubits long by the cubit and an hand breadth: so he measured the breadth of the building, one reed; and the height, one reed. Then came he unto the gate which looketh toward the east, and went up the stairs thereof...

And, behold, the glory of the God of Israel came from the way of the east: and his voice was like a noise of many waters: and the earth shined with his glory. And it was according to the appearance of the vision which I saw, even according to the vision that I saw when I came to destroy the city: and the visions were like the vision that I saw by the river Chebar; and I fell upon my face. And the glory of the Lord came into the house by the way of the gate whose prospect is toward the east. So the spirit took me up, and brought me into the inner court; and, behold, the glory of the Lord filled the house.

And I heard him speaking unto me out of the house; and the man stood by me. And he said unto me, Son of man, the place of my throne, and the place of the soles of my feet, where I will dwell in the midst of the children of Israel for ever, and my holy name, shall the house of Israel no more defile... Thou son of man, shew the house to the house of Israel, that they may be ashamed of their iniquities: and let them measure the pattern. And if they be ashamed of all that they have done, shew them the form of the house, and the fashion thereof, and the goings out thereof, and the comings in thereof, and all the forms thereof, and all the ordinances thereof, and all the forms thereof, and all the laws thereof: and write it in their sight, that they may keep the whole form thereof, and all the ordinances thereof, and do them...

Then he brought me back the way of the gate of the outward sanctuary which looketh toward the east; and it was shut. Then said the Lord unto me; This gate shall be shut, it shall not be opened, and no man shall enter in by it; because the Lord, the God of Israel, hath entered in by it, therefore it shall be shut. It is for the prince; the prince, he shall sit in it to eat bread before the Lord; he shall enter by the way of the porch of that gate, and shall go out by the way of the same. Then brought he me the way of the north gate before the house: and I looked, and, behold, the glory of the Lord filled the house of the Lord: and I fell upon my face...

Afterward he brought me again unto the door of the house; and, behold, waters issued out from under the threshold of the house eastward: for the forefront of the house stood toward the east, and the waters came down from under from the right side of the house, at the south side of the altar. Then brought he me out of the way of the gate northward, and led me about the way without unto the utter gate by the way that looketh eastward; and, behold, there ran out waters on the right side.

And when the man that had the line in his hand went forth eastward, he measured a thousand cubits, and he brought me through the waters; the waters were to the ankles. Again he measured a thousand, and brought me through the waters; the waters were to the knees. Again he measured a thousand, and brought me through; the waters were to the loins. Afterward he measured a thousand; and it was a river that I could not pass over: for the waters were risen, waters to swim in, a river that could not be passed over.

And he said unto me... by the river upon the bank thereof, on this side and on that side, shall grow all trees for meat, whose leaf shall not fade, neither shall the fruit thereof be consumed: it shall bring forth new fruit according to his months, because their waters they issued out of the sanctuary: and the fruit thereof shall be for meat, and the leaf thereof for medicine...

And these are the goings out of the city on the north side, four thousand and five hundred measures. And the gates of the city shall be after the names of the tribes of Israel: three gates northward; one gate of Reuben, one gate of Judah, one gate of Levi. And at the east side four thousand and five hundred: and three gates; and one gate of Joseph, one gate of Benjamin, one gate of Dan. And at the south side four thousand and five hundred measures: and three gates; one gate of Simeon, one gate of Issachar, one gate of Zebulun. At the west side four thousand and five hundred, with their three gates; one gate of Gad, one gate of Asher, one gate of Naphtali. It was round about eighteen thousand measures: and the name of the city from that day shall be, The Lord is there.

Lamentations

A PROPHET LAMENTS THE FALL OF JERUSALEM
Lamentations 1:1–12, 2:11–22, 3:18–48, 5:1–22

How doth the city sit solitary,
    that was full of people!
how is she become as a widow!
    she that was great among the nations,
and princess among the provinces,
    how is she become tributary!

She weepeth sore in the night,
    and her tears are on her cheeks:
among all her lovers
    she hath none to comfort her:
all her friends have dealt treacherously with her,
    they are become her enemies.

Judah is gone into captivity because of affliction,
    and because of great servitude:
she dwelleth among the heathen,
    she findeth no rest:
all her persecutors overtook her
    between the straits.

The ways of Zion do mourn,
    because none come to the solemn feasts:
all her gates are desolate:
    her priests sigh,
her virgins are afflicted,
    and she is in bitterness.

Her adversaries are the chief,
    her enemies prosper;
for the Lord hath afflicted her
    for the multitude of her transgressions:

her children are gone into captivity
    before the enemy.

And from the daughter of Zion
    all her beauty is departed:
her princes are become like harts
    that find no pasture,
and they are gone without strength
    before the pursuer.

Jerusalem remembered in the days of her affliction
    and of her miseries
all her pleasant things
    that she had in the days of old,
when her people fell into the hand of the enemy,
    and none did help her:
the adversaries saw her,
    and did mock at her sabbaths.

Jerusalem hath grievously sinned;
    therefore she is removed:
all that honoured her despise her,
    because they have seen her nakedness:
yea, she sigheth,
    and turneth backward.

Her filthiness is in her skirts;
    she remembereth not her last end;
therefore she came down wonderfully:
    she had no comforter.
O Lord, behold my affliction:
    for the enemy hath magnified himself.

The adversary hath spread out his hand
    upon all her pleasant things:
for she hath seen that the heathen
    entered into her sanctuary,
whom thou didst command
    that they should not enter into thy congregation.

All her people sigh,
    they seek bread;
they have given their pleasant things
    for meat to relieve the soul:
see, O Lord, and consider;
    for I am become vile.

Is it nothing to you, all ye that pass by?
    behold, and see
if there be any sorrow like unto my sorrow,
    which is done unto me,
wherewith the Lord hath afflicted me
    in the day of his fierce anger...

Mine eyes do fail with tears,
    my bowels are troubled,
my liver is poured upon the earth,
    for the destruction of the daughter of my people;
because the children and the sucklings swoon
    in the streets of the city.

They say to their mothers,
    Where is corn and wine?
when they swooned as the wounded
    in the streets of the city,
when their soul was poured out
    into their mothers' bosom.

What thing shall I take to witness for thee?
    what thing shall I liken to thee,
O daughter of Jerusalem?
    what shall I equal to thee,
that I may comfort thee,
    O virgin daughter of Zion?
for thy breach is great like the sea:
    who can heal thee?

Thy prophets have seen
    vain and foolish things for thee:

and they have not discovered thine iniquity,
    to turn away thy captivity;
but have seen for thee false burdens
    and causes of banishment.

All that pass by
    clap their hands at thee;
they hiss and wag their head
    at the daughter of Jerusalem, saying,
Is this the city that men call
    The perfection of beauty,
    The joy of the whole earth?

All thine enemies
    have opened their mouth against thee:
they hiss and gnash the teeth:
    they say,
We have swallowed her up:
    certainly this is the day that we looked for;
    we have found, we have seen it.

The Lord hath done that which he had devised;
    he hath fulfilled his word
    that he had commanded in the days of old:
he hath thrown down,
    and hath not pitied:
and he hath caused thine enemy to rejoice over thee,
    he hath set up the horn of thine adversaries.

Their heart cried unto the Lord,
    O wall of the daughter of Zion,
let tears run down like a river
    day and night:
give thyself no rest;
    let not the apple of thine eye cease.
Arise, cry out in the night:
    in the beginning of the watches
pour out thine heart like water
    before the face of the Lord:

lift up thy hands toward him
for the life of thy young children,
that faint for hunger
in the top of every street.

Behold, O Lord, and consider
to whom thou hast done this.
Shall the women eat their fruit,
and children of a span long?
shall the priest and the prophet be slain
in the sanctuary of the Lord?

The young and the old
lie on the ground in the streets:
my virgins and my young men
are fallen by the sword;
thou hast slain them in the day of thine anger;
thou hast killed, and not pitied.

Thou hast called as in a solemn day
my terrors round about,
so that in the day of the Lord's anger
none escaped nor remained:
those that I have swaddled and brought up
hath mine enemy consumed…

And I said, My strength and my hope
is perished from the Lord:
Remembering mine affliction and my misery,
the wormwood and the gall.
My soul hath them still in remembrance,
and is humbled in me.
This I recall to my mind,
therefore have I hope.

It is of the Lord's mercies
that we are not consumed,
because his compassions fail not.
They are new every morning:
great is thy faithfulness.

The Lord is my portion, saith my soul;
  therefore will I hope in him.

The Lord is good unto them that wait for him,
  to the soul that seeketh him.
It is good that a man should both hope
  and quietly wait for the salvation of the Lord.
It is good for a man
  that he bear the yoke in his youth.
He sitteth alone and keepeth silence,
  because he hath borne it upon him.
He putteth his mouth in the dust;
  if so be there may be hope.
He giveth his cheek to him that smiteth him:
  he is filled full with reproach.

For the Lord will not cast off for ever:
But though he cause grief,
  yet will he have compassion
  according to the multitude of his mercies.
For he doth not afflict willingly
  nor grieve the children of men.

To crush under his feet
  all the prisoners of the earth,
To turn aside the right of a man
  before the face of the most High,
To subvert a man in his cause,
  the Lord approveth not.

Who is he that saith, and it cometh to pass,
  when the Lord commandeth it not?
Out of the mouth of the most High
  proceedeth not evil and good?
Wherefore doth a living man complain,
  a man for the punishment of his sins?
Let us search and try our ways,
  and turn again to the Lord.
Let us lift up our heart with our hands
  unto God in the heavens.

We have transgressed and have rebelled:
    thou hast not pardoned.
Thou hast covered with anger, and persecuted us:
    thou hast slain, thou hast not pitied.
Thou hast covered thyself with a cloud,
    that our prayer should not pass through.
Thou hast made us as the offscouring
    and refuse in the midst of the people.

All our enemies
    have opened their mouths against us.
Fear and a snare is come upon us,
    desolation and destruction.
Mine eye runneth down with rivers of water
    for the destruction of the daughter of my people…

Remember, O Lord, what is come upon us:
    consider, and behold our reproach.
Our inheritance is turned to strangers,
    our houses to aliens.
We are orphans and fatherless,
    our mothers are as widows.
We have drunken our water for money;
    our wood is sold unto us.
Our necks are under persecution:
    we labour, and have no rest.
We have given the hand to the Egyptians,
    and to the Assyrians, to be satisfied with bread.
Our fathers have sinned, and are not;
    and we have borne their iniquities.
Servants have ruled over us:
    there is none that doth deliver us out of their hand.
We gat our bread with the peril of our lives
    because of the sword of the wilderness.
Our skin was black like an oven
    because of the terrible famine.
They ravished the women in Zion,
    and the maids in the cities of Judah.

Princes are hanged up by their hand:
    the faces of elders were not honoured.
They took the young men to grind,
    and the children fell under the wood.
The elders have ceased from the gate,
    the young men from their musick.
The joy of our heart is ceased;
    our dance is turned into mourning.
The crown is fallen from our head:
    woe unto us, that we have sinned!
For this our heart is faint;
    for these things our eyes are dim.
Because of the mountain of Zion,
    which is desolate, the foxes walk upon it.

Thou, O Lord, remainest for ever;
    thy throne from generation to generation.
Wherefore dost thou forget us for ever,
    and forsake us so long time?
Turn thou us unto thee, O Lord,
    and we shall be turned;
    renew our days as of old.
But thou hast utterly rejected us;
    thou art very wroth against us.

Obadiah

GOD'S JUDGMENT ON EDOM
Obadiah 1:1–4, 8–17, 21

The vision of Obadiah.

Thus saith the Lord God concerning Edom;

We have heard a rumour from the Lord,
    and an ambassador is sent among the heathen,
Arise ye, and let us rise up against her in battle.

Behold, I have made thee small among the heathen:
    thou art greatly despised.
The pride of thine heart hath deceived thee,
    thou that dwellest in the clefts of the rock,
    whose habitation is high;
that saith in his heart,
    Who shall bring me down to the ground?
Though thou exalt thyself as the eagle,
    and though thou set thy nest among the stars,
    thence will I bring thee down,
        saith the Lord...

Shall I not in that day,
    saith the Lord,
    even destroy the wise men out of Edom,
and understanding out of the mount of Esau?
And thy mighty men, O Teman, shall be dismayed,
    to the end that every one of the mount of Esau
    may be cut off by slaughter.
For thy violence against thy brother Jacob
    shame shall cover thee,
    and thou shalt be cut off for ever.

In the day that thou stoodest on the other side,
    in the day that the strangers carried away captive his forces,
and foreigners entered into his gates,
    and cast lots upon Jerusalem,
    even thou wast as one of them.
But thou shouldest not have looked
    on the day of thy brother
    in the day that he became a stranger;
neither shouldest thou have rejoiced
    over the children of Judah
    in the day of their destruction;
neither shouldest thou have spoken proudly
    in the day of distress.
Thou shouldest not have entered
    into the gate of my people
    in the day of their calamity;
yea, thou shouldest not have looked
    on their affliction in the day of their calamity,
nor have laid hands on their substance
    in the day of their calamity;
Neither shouldest thou have stood in the crossway,
    to cut off those of his that did escape;
neither shouldest thou have delivered up
    those of his that did remain in the day of distress.

For the day of the Lord is near upon all the heathen:
    as thou hast done, it shall be done unto thee:
    thy reward shall return upon thine own head.
For as ye have drunk upon my holy mountain,
    so shall all the heathen drink continually,
yea, they shall drink, and they shall swallow down,
    and they shall be as though they had not been.

But upon mount Zion shall be deliverance,
    and there shall be holiness;
and the house of Jacob
    shall possess their possessions...

And saviours shall come up on mount Zion
    to judge the mount of Esau;
and the kingdom shall be the Lord's.

Second Isaiah

THE CONSOLATION OF ISRAEL
Isaiah 40:1–31

Comfort ye, comfort ye my people,
    saith your God.
Speak ye comfortably to Jerusalem, and cry unto her,
    that her warfare is accomplished,
    that her iniquity is pardoned:
for she hath received of the Lord's hand
    double for all her sins.

The voice of him that crieth in the wilderness,
Prepare ye the way of the Lord,
    make straight in the desert a highway for our God.
Every valley shall be exalted,
    and every mountain and hill shall be made low:
and the crooked shall be made straight,
    and the rough places plain:
And the glory of the Lord shall be revealed,
    and all flesh shall see it together:
    for the mouth of the Lord hath spoken it.

The voice said, Cry.
    And he said, What shall I cry?
All flesh is grass,
    and all the goodliness thereof
    is as the flower of the field:
The grass withereth, the flower fadeth:
    because the spirit of the Lord bloweth upon it:
    surely the people is grass.
The grass withereth, the flower fadeth:
    but the word of our God shall stand for ever.

O Zion, that bringest good tidings,
    get thee up into the high mountain;
O Jerusalem, that bringest good tidings,
    lift up thy voice with strength;
lift it up, be not afraid;
    say unto the cities of Judah,
    Behold your God!
Behold, the Lord God will come with strong hand,
    and his arm shall rule for him:
behold, his reward is with him,
    and his work before him.
He shall feed his flock like a shepherd:
    he shall gather the lambs with his arm,
and carry them in his bosom,
    and shall gently lead those that are with young.

Who hath measured the waters in the hollow of his hand,
    and meted out heaven with the span,
and comprehended the dust of the earth in a measure,
    and weighed the mountains in scales,
    and the hills in a balance?
Who hath directed the Spirit of the Lord,
    or being his counsellor hath taught him?
With whom took he counsel, and who instructed him,
    and taught him in the path of judgment,
and taught him knowledge,
    and shewed to him the way of understanding?
Behold, the nations are as a drop of a bucket,
    and are counted as the small dust of the balance:
behold, he taketh up the isles
    as a very little thing.
And Lebanon is not sufficient to burn,
    nor the beasts thereof sufficient for a burnt offering.
All nations before him are as nothing;
    and they are counted to him less than nothing, and vanity.

To whom then will ye liken God?
    or what likeness will ye compare unto him?

The workman melteth a graven image,
    and the goldsmith spreadeth it over with gold,
    and casteth silver chains.
He that is so impoverished that he hath no oblation
    chooseth a tree that will not rot;
he seeketh unto him a cunning workman
    to prepare a graven image, that shall not be moved.

Have ye not known?
    have ye not heard?
hath it not been told you from the beginning?
    have ye not understood from the foundations of the earth?
It is he that sitteth upon the circle of the earth,
    and the inhabitants thereof are as grasshoppers;
that stretcheth out the heavens as a curtain,
    and spreadeth them out as a tent to dwell in:
That bringeth the princes to nothing;
    he maketh the judges of the earth as vanity.
Yea, they shall not be planted;
    yea, they shall not be sown:
    yea, their stock shall not take root in the earth:
and he shall also blow upon them,
    and they shall wither,
    and the whirlwind shall take them away as stubble.

To whom then will ye liken me, or shall I be equal?
    saith the Holy One.
Lift up your eyes on high,
    and behold who hath created these things,
    that bringeth out their host by number:
he calleth them all by names by the greatness of his might,
    for that he is strong in power; not one faileth.

Why sayest thou, O Jacob, and speakest, O Israel,
    My way is hid from the Lord,
    and my judgment is passed over from my God?
Hast thou not known?
    hast thou not heard,

that the everlasting God, the Lord,
    the Creator of the ends of the earth,
fainteth not, neither is weary?
    there is no searching of his understanding.
He giveth power to the faint;
    and to them that have no might he increaseth strength.
Even the youths shall faint and be weary,
    and the young men shall utterly fall:
But they that wait upon the Lord shall renew their strength;
    they shall mount up with wings as eagles;
they shall run, and not be weary;
    and they shall walk, and not faint.

GOD'S SUFFERING SERVANT: THE FIRST SONG
Isaiah 42:1–9

Behold my servant, whom I uphold;
    mine elect, in whom my soul delighteth;
I have put my spirit upon him:
    he shall bring forth judgment to the Gentiles.
He shall not cry, nor lift up,
    nor cause his voice to be heard in the street.
A bruised reed shall he not break,
    and the smoking flax shall he not quench:
    he shall bring forth judgment unto truth.
He shall not fail nor be discouraged,
    till he have set judgment in the earth:
    and the isles shall wait for his law.

Thus saith God the Lord,
    he that created the heavens,
    and stretched them out;
he that spread forth the earth,
    and that which cometh out of it;
he that giveth breath unto the people upon it,
    and spirit to them that walk therein:

I the Lord have called thee in righteousness,
   and will hold thine hand, and will keep thee,
and give thee for a covenant of the people,
   for a light of the Gentiles;
To open the blind eyes,
   to bring out the prisoners from the prison,
   and them that sit in darkness out of the prison house.

I am the Lord: that is my name:
   and my glory will I not give to another,
   neither my praise to graven images.
Behold, the former things are come to pass,
   and new things do I declare:
   before they spring forth I tell you of them.

GOD'S SUFFERING SERVANT: THE SECOND SONG
Isaiah 49:1–6

Listen, O isles, unto me;
   and hearken, ye people, from far;
The Lord hath called me from the womb;
   from the bowels of my mother
   hath he made mention of my name.
And he hath made my mouth like a sharp sword;
   in the shadow of his hand hath he hid me,
and made me a polished shaft;
   in his quiver hath he hid me;
And said unto me, Thou art my servant, O Israel,
   in whom I will be glorified.
Then I said, I have laboured in vain,
   I have spent my strength for nought, and in vain:
yet surely my judgment is with the Lord,
   and my work with my God.

And now, saith the Lord that formed me from the womb
   to be his servant,
   to bring Jacob again to him,

Though Israel be not gathered,
  yet shall I be glorious in the eyes of the Lord,
  and my God shall be my strength.
And he said, It is a light thing
  that thou shouldest be my servant
to raise up the tribes of Jacob,
  and to restore the preserved of Israel:
I will also give thee for a light to the Gentiles,
  that thou mayest be my salvation
  unto the end of the earth.

GOD'S SUFFERING SERVANT: THE THIRD SONG
Isaiah 50:4–11

The Lord God hath given me the tongue of the learned,
  that I should know how to speak a word in season
  to him that is weary:
he wakeneth morning by morning,
  he wakeneth mine ear to hear as the learned.
The Lord God hath opened mine ear,
  and I was not rebellious, neither turned away back.
I gave my back to the smiters,
  and my cheeks to them that plucked off the hair:
I hid not my face
  from shame and spitting.
For the Lord God will help me;
  therefore shall I not be confounded:
therefore have I set my face like a flint,
  and I know that I shall not be ashamed.
He is near that justifieth me;
  who will contend with me?
let us stand together:
  who is mine adversary?
let him come near to me.
Behold, the Lord God will help me;
  who is he that shall condemn me?

lo, they all shall wax old as a garment;
   the moth shall eat them up.

Who is among you that feareth the Lord,
   that obeyeth the voice of his servant,
that walketh in darkness,
   and hath no light?
let him trust in the name of the Lord,
   and stay upon his God.
Behold, all ye that kindle a fire,
   that compass yourselves about with sparks:
walk in the light of your fire,
   and in the sparks that ye have kindled.
This shall ye have of mine hand;
   ye shall lie down in sorrow.

GOD'S SUFFERING SERVANT: THE FOURTH SONG
Isaiah 52:13 – 53:12

Behold, my servant shall deal prudently,
   he shall be exalted and extolled, and be very high.
As many were astonied at thee;
   his visage was so marred more than any man,
   and his form more than the sons of men:
So shall he sprinkle many nations;
   the kings shall shut their mouths at him:
for that which had not been told them shall they see;
   and that which they had not heard shall they consider.

Who hath believed our report?
   and to whom is the arm of the Lord revealed?
For he shall grow up before him as a tender plant,
   and as a root out of a dry ground:
he hath no form nor comeliness;
   and when we shall see him,
   there is no beauty that we should desire him.

171

He is despised and rejected of men;
   a man of sorrows, and acquainted with grief:
and we hid as it were our faces from him;
   he was despised, and we esteemed him not.

Surely he hath borne our griefs, and carried our sorrows:
   yet we did esteem him stricken, smitten of God, and afflicted.
But he was wounded for our transgressions,
   he was bruised for our iniquities:
the chastisement of our peace was upon him;
   and with his stripes we are healed.
All we like sheep have gone astray;
   we have turned every one to his own way;
   and the Lord hath laid on him the iniquity of us all.

He was oppressed, and he was afflicted,
   yet he opened not his mouth:
he is brought as a lamb to the slaughter,
   and as a sheep before her shearers is dumb,
   so he openeth not his mouth.
He was taken from prison and from judgment:
   and who shall declare his generation?
for he was cut off out of the land of the living:
   for the transgression of my people was he stricken.
And he made his grave with the wicked,
   and with the rich in his death;
because he had done no violence,
   neither was any deceit in his mouth.
Yet it pleased the Lord to bruise him;
   he hath put him to grief:
when thou shalt make his soul an offering for sin,
   he shall see his seed,
he shall prolong his days,
   and the pleasure of the Lord shall prosper in his hand.
He shall see of the travail of his soul,
   and shall be satisfied:
by his knowledge shall my righteous servant justify many;
   for he shall bear their iniquities.

Therefore will I divide him a portion with the great,
    and he shall divide the spoil with the strong;
because he hath poured out his soul unto death:
    and he was numbered with the transgressors;
and he bare the sin of many,
    and made intercession for the transgressors.

GOD'S EVERLASTING MERCY
Isaiah 55

Ho, every one that thirsteth,
    come ye to the waters,
and he that hath no money;
    come ye, buy, and eat;
yea, come, buy wine and milk
    without money and without price.
Wherefore do ye spend money for that which is not bread?
    and your labour for that which satisfieth not?
hearken diligently unto me, and eat ye that which is good,
    and let your soul delight itself in fatness.
Incline your ear, and come unto me:
    hear, and your soul shall live;
and I will make an everlasting covenant with you,
    even the sure mercies of David.
Behold, I have given him for a witness to the people,
    a leader and commander to the people.
Behold, thou shalt call a nation that thou knowest not,
    and nations that knew not thee
shall run unto thee because of the Lord thy God,
    and for the Holy One of Israel;
    for he hath glorified thee.

Seek ye the Lord while he may be found,
    call ye upon him while he is near:
Let the wicked forsake his way,
    and the unrighteous man his thoughts:

and let him return unto the Lord,
    and he will have mercy upon him;
and to our God,
    for he will abundantly pardon.
For my thoughts are not your thoughts,
    neither are your ways my ways,
        saith the Lord.
For as the heavens are higher than the earth,
    so are my ways higher than your ways,
    and my thoughts than your thoughts.
For as the rain cometh down, and the snow from heaven,
    and returneth not thither, but watereth the earth,
and maketh it bring forth and bud,
    that it may give seed to the sower,
    and bread to the eater:
So shall my word be that goeth forth out of my mouth:
    it shall not return unto me void,
but it shall accomplish that which I please,
    and it shall prosper in the thing whereto I sent it.
For ye shall go out with joy,
    and be led forth with peace:
the mountains and the hills
    shall break forth before you into singing,
and all the trees of the field
    shall clap their hands.
Instead of the thorn shall come up the fir tree,
    and instead of the brier shall come up the myrtle tree:
and it shall be to the Lord for a name,
    for an everlasting sign that shall not be cut off.

PROPHETS
AFTER THE EXILE

Haggai

GOD CALLS HIS PEOPLE TO REBUILD THE TEMPLE
Haggai 1:1–12, 2:1–10, 21–23

In the second year of Darius the king, in the sixth month, in the first day of the month, came the word of the Lord by Haggai the prophet unto Zerubbabel the son of Shealtiel, governor of Judah, and to Joshua the son of Josedech, the high priest, saying, Thus speaketh the Lord of hosts, saying, This people say, The time is not come, the time that the Lord's house should be built.

Then came the word of the Lord by Haggai the prophet, saying, Is it time for you, O ye, to dwell in your cieled houses, and this house lie waste?

Now therefore thus saith the Lord of hosts; Consider your ways. Ye have sown much, and bring in little; ye eat, but ye have not enough; ye drink, but ye are not filled with drink; ye clothe you, but there is none warm; and he that earneth wages earneth wages to put it into a bag with holes.

Thus saith the Lord of hosts; Consider your ways. Go up to the mountain, and bring wood, and build the house; and I will take pleasure in it, and I will be glorified, saith the Lord. Ye looked for much, and, lo it came to little; and when ye brought it home, I did blow upon it. Why? saith the Lord of hosts. Because of mine house that is waste, and ye run every man unto his own house. Therefore the heaven over you is stayed from dew, and the earth is stayed from her fruit. And I called for a drought upon the land, and upon the mountains, and upon the corn, and upon the new wine, and upon the oil, and upon that which the ground bringeth forth, and upon men, and upon cattle, and upon all the labour of the hands.

Then Zerubbabel the son of Shealtiel, and Joshua the son of Josedech, the high priest, with all the remnant of the people, obeyed the voice of the Lord their God, and the words of Haggai the prophet, as the Lord their God had sent him, and the people did fear before the Lord...

In the seventh month, in the one and twentieth day of the month, came the word of the Lord by the prophet Haggai, saying, Speak now to Zerubbabel the son of Shealtiel, governor of Judah, and to Joshua the son of Josedech, the high priest, and to the residue of the people, saying, Who is left among you that saw this house in her first glory? and how do ye see it now? is it not in your eyes in comparison of it as nothing? Yet now be strong, O Zerubbabel, saith the Lord; and be strong, O Joshua, son of Josedech, the high priest; and be strong, all ye people of the land, saith the Lord, and work: for I am with you, saith the Lord of hosts: According to the word that I covenanted with you when ye came out of Egypt, so my spirit remaineth among you: fear ye not.

For thus saith the Lord of hosts; Yet once, it is a little while, and I will shake the heavens, and the earth, and the sea, and the dry land; And I will shake all nations, and the desire of all nations shall come: and I will fill this house with glory, saith the Lord of hosts. The silver is mine, and the gold is mine, saith the Lord of hosts. The glory of this latter house shall be greater than of the former, saith the Lord of hosts: and in this place will I give peace, saith the Lord of hosts.

In the four and twentieth day of the ninth month, in the second year of Darius, came the word of the Lord by Haggai the prophet, saying… Speak to Zerubbabel, governor of Judah, saying, I will shake the heavens and the earth; And I will overthrow the throne of kingdoms, and I will destroy the strength of the kingdoms of the heathen; and I will overthrow the chariots, and those that ride in them; and the horses and their riders shall come down, every one by the sword of his brother. In that day, saith the Lord of hosts, will I take thee, O Zerubbabel, my servant, the son of Shealtiel, saith the Lord, and will make thee as a signet: for I have chosen thee, saith the Lord of hosts.

Zechariah

GOD CALLS HIS PEOPLE TO REPENTANCE
Zechariah 1:1–6

In the eighth month, in the second year of Darius, came the word of the Lord unto Zechariah, the son of Berechiah, the son of Iddo the prophet, saying, The Lord hath been sore displeased with your fathers.

Therefore say thou unto them, Thus saith the Lord of hosts; Turn ye unto me, saith the Lord of hosts, and I will turn unto you, saith the Lord of hosts. Be ye not as your fathers, unto whom the former prophets have cried, saying, Thus saith the Lord of hosts; Turn ye now from your evil ways, and from your evil doings: but they did not hear, nor hearken unto me, saith the Lord. Your fathers, where are they? and the prophets, do they live for ever? But my words and my statutes, which I commanded my servants the prophets, did they not take hold of your fathers? and they returned and said, Like as the Lord of hosts thought to do unto us, according to our ways, and according to our doings, so hath he dealt with us.

THE VISION OF THE HORSEMEN
Zechariah 1:7–17

Upon the four and twentieth day of the eleventh month, which is the month Sebat, in the second year of Darius, came the word of the Lord unto Zechariah, the son of Berechiah, the son of Iddo the prophet, saying, I saw by night, and behold a man riding upon a red horse, and he stood among the myrtle trees that were in the bottom; and behind him were there red horses, speckled, and white.

Then said I, O my lord, what are these? And the angel that talked with me said unto me, I will shew thee what these be.

And the man that stood among the myrtle trees answered and

said, These are they whom the Lord hath sent to walk to and fro through the earth. And they answered the angel of the Lord that stood among the myrtle trees, and said, We have walked to and fro through the earth, and, behold, all the earth sitteth still, and is at rest.

Then the angel of the Lord answered and said, O Lord of hosts, how long wilt thou not have mercy on Jerusalem and on the cities of Judah, against which thou hast had indignation these threescore and ten years? And the Lord answered the angel that talked with me with good words and comfortable words.

So the angel that communed with me said unto me, Cry thou, saying, Thus saith the Lord of hosts; I am jealous for Jerusalem and for Zion with a great jealousy. And I am very sore displeased with the heathen that are at ease: for I was but a little displeased, and they helped forward the affliction.

Therefore thus saith the Lord; I am returned to Jerusalem with mercies: my house shall be built in it, saith the Lord of hosts, and a line shall be stretched forth upon Jerusalem.

Cry yet, saying, Thus saith the Lord of hosts; My cities through prosperity shall yet be spread abroad; and the Lord shall yet comfort Zion, and shall yet choose Jerusalem.

THE VISION OF THE MAN
WITH A MEASURING LINE
Zechariah 2:1–5

I lifted up mine eyes again, and looked, and behold a man with a measuring line in his hand. Then said I, Whither goest thou? And he said unto me, To measure Jerusalem, to see what is the breadth thereof, and what is the length thereof.

And, behold, the angel that talked with me went forth, and another angel went out to meet him, and said unto him, Run, speak to this young man, saying, Jerusalem shall be inhabited as towns without walls for the multitude of men and cattle therein: For I, saith the Lord, will be unto her a wall of fire round about, and will be the glory in the midst of her.

THE VISION OF SATAN AND THE ANGEL
Zechariah 3

And he shewed me Joshua the high priest standing before the angel of the Lord, and Satan standing at his right hand to resist him. And the Lord said unto Satan, The Lord rebuke thee, O Satan; even the Lord that hath chosen Jerusalem rebuke thee: is not this a brand plucked out of the fire?

Now Joshua was clothed with filthy garments, and stood before the angel. And he answered and spake unto those that stood before him, saying, Take away the filthy garments from him. And unto him he said, Behold, I have caused thine iniquity to pass from thee, and I will clothe thee with change of raiment. And I said, Let them set a fair mitre upon his head. So they set a fair mitre upon his head, and clothed him with garments. And the angel of the Lord stood by.

And the angel of the Lord protested unto Joshua, saying, Thus saith the Lord of hosts; If thou wilt walk in my ways, and if thou wilt keep my charge, then thou shalt also judge my house, and shalt also keep my courts, and I will give thee places to walk among these that stand by.

Hear now, O Joshua the high priest, thou, and thy fellows that sit before thee: for they are men wondered at: for, behold, I will bring forth my servant the Branch. For behold the stone that I have laid before Joshua; upon one stone shall be seven eyes: behold, I will engrave the graving thereof, saith the Lord of hosts, and I will remove the iniquity of that land in one day.

In that day, saith the Lord of hosts, shall ye call every man his neighbour under the vine and under the fig tree.

THE VISION OF THE CANDLESTICK
AND OLIVE TREES
Zechariah 4

And the angel that talked with me came again, and waked me, as a man that is wakened out of his sleep. And said unto me, What seest thou? And I said, I have looked, and behold a candlestick all of gold, with a bowl upon the top of it, and his seven lamps thereon, and seven pipes to the seven lamps, which are upon the top thereof: And two olive trees by it, one upon the right side of the bowl, and the other upon the left side thereof.

So I answered and spake to the angel that talked with me, saying, What are these, my lord? Then the angel that talked with me answered and said unto me, Knowest thou not what these be? And I said, No, my lord.

Then he answered and spake unto me, saying, This is the word of the Lord unto Zerubbabel, saying, Not by might, nor by power, but by my spirit, saith the Lord of hosts. Who art thou, O great mountain? before Zerubbabel thou shalt become a plain: and he shall bring forth the headstone thereof with shoutings, crying, Grace, grace unto it.

Moreover the word of the Lord came unto me, saying, The hands of Zerubbabel have laid the foundation of this house; his hands shall also finish it; and thou shalt know that the Lord of hosts hath sent me unto you.

For who hath despised the day of small things? for they shall rejoice, and shall see the plummet in the hand of Zerubbabel with those seven; they are the eyes of the Lord, which run to and fro through the whole earth.

Then answered I, and said unto him, What are these two olive trees upon the right side of the candlestick and upon the left side thereof? And I answered again, and said unto him, What be these two olive branches which through the two golden pipes empty the golden oil out of themselves?

And he answered me and said, Knowest thou not what these be? And I said, No, my lord. Then said he, These are the two anointed ones, that stand by the Lord of the whole earth.

THE CRIME AND THE PUNISHMENT
Zechariah 7:8–14

And the word of the Lord came unto Zechariah, saying, Thus speaketh the Lord of hosts, saying, Execute true judgment, and shew mercy and compassions every man to his brother: And oppress not the widow, nor the fatherless, the stranger, nor the poor; and let none of you imagine evil against his brother in your heart.

But they refused to hearken, and pulled away the shoulder, and stopped their ears, that they should not hear. Yea, they made their hearts as an adamant stone, lest they should hear the law, and the words which the Lord of hosts hath sent in his spirit by the former prophets: therefore came a great wrath from the Lord of hosts.

Therefore it is come to pass, that as he cried, and they would not hear; so they cried, and I would not hear, saith the Lord of hosts: But I scattered them with a whirlwind among all the nations whom they knew not. Thus the land was desolate after them, that no man passed through nor returned: for they laid the pleasant land desolate.

THE COMING OF ZION'S KING
Zechariah 9:9–10

Rejoice greatly, O daughter of Zion;
    shout, O daughter of Jerusalem:
behold, thy King cometh unto thee:
    he is just, and having salvation;
lowly, and riding upon an ass,
    and upon a colt the foal of an ass.
And I will cut off the chariot from Ephraim,
    and the horse from Jerusalem,
and the battle bow shall be cut off:
    and he shall speak peace unto the heathen:
and his dominion shall be from sea even to sea,
    and from the river even to the ends of the earth.

GOD WILL SAVE THE HOUSE OF DAVID
Zechariah 12:8–10, 13:1–9

In that day shall the Lord defend the inhabitants of Jerusalem; and he that is feeble among them at that day shall be as David; and the house of David shall be as God, as the angel of the Lord before them. And it shall come to pass in that day, that I will seek to destroy all the nations that come against Jerusalem.

And I will pour upon the house of David, and upon the inhabitants of Jerusalem, the spirit of grace and of supplications: and they shall look upon me whom they have pierced, and they shall mourn for him, as one mourneth for his only son, and shall be in bitterness for him, as one that is in bitterness for his firstborn...

In that day there shall be a fountain opened to the house of David and to the inhabitants of Jerusalem for sin and for uncleanness.

And it shall come to pass in that day, saith the Lord of hosts, that I will cut off the names of the idols out of the land, and they shall no more be remembered: and also I will cause the prophets and the unclean spirit to pass out of the land. And it shall come to pass, that when any shall yet prophesy, then his father and his mother that begat him shall say unto him, Thou shalt not live; for thou speakest lies in the name of the Lord: and his father and his mother that begat him shall thrust him through when he prophesieth.

And it shall come to pass in that day, that the prophets shall be ashamed every one of his vision, when he hath prophesied; neither shall they wear a rough garment to deceive: But he shall say, I am no prophet, I am an husbandman; for man taught me to keep cattle from my youth. And one shall say unto him, What are these wounds in thine hands? Then he shall answer, Those with which I was wounded in the house of my friends.

Awake, O sword, against my shepherd,
   and against the man that is my fellow,
      saith the Lord of hosts:
smite the shepherd, and the sheep shall be scattered:
   and I will turn mine hand upon the little ones.
And it shall come to pass, that in all the land,
      saith the Lord,
   two parts therein shall be cut off and die;
   but the third shall be left therein.
And I will bring the third part through the fire,
   and will refine them as silver is refined,
   and will try them as gold is tried:

> they shall call on my name,
>   and I will hear them:
> I will say, It is my people:
>   and they shall say, The Lord is my God.

THE FINAL VICTORY
Zechariah 14:1–9, 16–21

Behold, the day of the Lord cometh, and thy spoil shall be divided in the midst of thee.

For I will gather all nations against Jerusalem to battle; and the city shall be taken, and the houses rifled, and the women ravished; and half of the city shall go forth into captivity, and the residue of the people shall not be cut off from the city.

Then shall the Lord go forth, and fight against those nations, as when he fought in the day of battle. And his feet shall stand in that day upon the mount of Olives, which is before Jerusalem on the east, and the mount of Olives shall cleave in the midst thereof toward the east and toward the west, and there shall be a very great valley; and half of the mountain shall remove toward the north, and half of it toward the south. And ye shall flee to the valley of the mountains; for the valley of the mountains shall reach unto Azal: yea, ye shall flee, like as ye fled from before the earthquake in the days of Uzziah king of Judah: and the Lord my God shall come, and all the saints with thee.

And it shall come to pass in that day, that the light shall not be clear, nor dark: but it shall be one day which shall be known to the Lord, not day, nor night: but it shall come to pass, that at evening time it shall be light.

And it shall be in that day, that living waters shall go out from Jerusalem; half of them toward the former sea, and half of them toward the hinder sea: in summer and in winter shall it be. And the Lord shall be king over all the earth: in that day shall there be one Lord, and his name one...

And it shall come to pass, that every one that is left of all the nations which came against Jerusalem shall even go up from year to year to worship the King, the Lord of hosts, and to keep the feast of tabernacles. And it shall be, that whoso will not come up of all the families of the earth unto Jerusalem to worship the King, the Lord of hosts, even upon them shall be no rain. And if the family of Egypt go not up, and come not, that have no rain; there shall be the plague, wherewith the Lord will smite the heathen that come not up to keep the feast of tabernacles. This shall be the punishment of Egypt, and the punishment of all nations that come not up to keep the feast of tabernacles.

In that day shall there be upon the bells of the horses, Holiness Unto the Lord; and the pots in the Lord's house shall be like the bowls before the altar. Yea, every pot in Jerusalem and in Judah shall be holiness unto the Lord of hosts: and all they that sacrifice shall come and take of them, and seethe therein: and in that day there shall be no more the Canaanite in the house of the Lord of hosts.

Third Isaiah

A HOUSE OF PRAYER FOR ALL PEOPLE
Isaiah 56:1–8

Thus saith the Lord,

Keep ye judgment, and do justice:
  for my salvation is near to come,
  and my righteousness to be revealed.
Blessed is the man that doeth this,
  and the son of man that layeth hold on it;
that keepeth the sabbath from polluting it,
  and keepeth his hand from doing any evil.
Neither let the son of the stranger,
  that hath joined himself to the Lord,
speak, saying,
  The Lord hath utterly separated me from his people:
neither let the eunuch say,
  Behold, I am a dry tree.

For thus saith the Lord unto the eunuchs that keep my sabbaths, and choose the things that please me, and take hold of my covenant;

Even unto them will I give in mine house and within my walls
  a place and a name better than of sons and of daughters:
I will give them an everlasting name,
  that shall not be cut off.
Also the sons of the stranger, that join themselves to the Lord,
  to serve him, and to love the name of the Lord,
  to be his servants,
every one that keepeth the sabbath from polluting it,
  and taketh hold of my covenant;
Even them will I bring to my holy mountain,
  and make them joyful in my house of prayer:

their burnt offerings and their sacrifices
    shall be accepted upon mine altar;
for mine house shall be called
    an house of prayer for all people.
The Lord God which gathereth the outcasts of Israel saith,
    Yet will I gather others to him,
      beside those that are gathered unto him.

HEALING PEACE
Isaiah 57:15–21

For thus saith the high and lofty One
    that inhabiteth eternity, whose name is Holy;
I dwell in the high and holy place,
    with him also that is of a contrite and humble spirit,
to revive the spirit of the humble,
    and to revive the heart of the contrite ones.
For I will not contend for ever,
    neither will I be always wroth:
for the spirit should fail before me,
    and the souls which I have made.
For the iniquity of his covetousness was I wroth,
    and smote him:
I hid me, and was wroth,
    and he went on frowardly in the way of his heart.
I have seen his ways,
    and will heal him:
I will lead him also,
    and restore comforts unto him and to his mourners.
I create the fruit of the lips;
    Peace, peace to him that is far off,
    and to him that is near, saith the Lord,
    and I will heal him.
But the wicked are like the troubled sea, when it cannot rest,
    whose waters cast up mire and dirt.
There is no peace, saith my God, to the wicked.

TRUE FASTING
Isaiah 58

Cry aloud, spare not, lift up thy voice like a trumpet,
  and shew my people their transgression,
  and the house of Jacob their sins.
Yet they seek me daily, and delight to know my ways,
  as a nation that did righteousness,
  and forsook not the ordinance of their God:
they ask of me the ordinances of justice;
  they take delight in approaching to God.
Wherefore have we fasted, say they, and thou seest not?
  wherefore have we afflicted our soul,
  and thou takest no knowledge?
Behold, in the day of your fast ye find pleasure,
  and exact all your labours.

Behold, ye fast for strife and debate,
  and to smite with the fist of wickedness:
ye shall not fast as ye do this day,
  to make your voice to be heard on high.
Is it such a fast that I have chosen?
  a day for a man to afflict his soul?
is it to bow down his head as a bulrush,
  and to spread sackcloth and ashes under him?
wilt thou call this a fast,
  and an acceptable day to the Lord?

Is not this the fast that I have chosen?
  to loose the bands of wickedness,
to undo the heavy burdens, and to let the oppressed go free,
  and that ye break every yoke?
Is it not to deal thy bread to the hungry,
  and that thou bring the poor that are cast out to thy house?
when thou seest the naked, that thou cover him;
  and that thou hide not thyself from thine own flesh?
Then shall thy light break forth as the morning,
  and thine health shall spring forth speedily:

and thy righteousness shall go before thee;
  the glory of the Lord shall be thy rereward.
Then shalt thou call, and the Lord shall answer;
  thou shalt cry, and he shall say, Here I am.
If thou take away from the midst of thee the yoke,
  the putting forth of the finger, and speaking vanity;
And if thou draw out thy soul to the hungry,
  and satisfy the afflicted soul;
then shall thy light rise in obscurity,
  and thy darkness be as the noonday:
And the Lord shall guide thee continually,
  and satisfy thy soul in drought, and make fat thy bones:
and thou shalt be like a watered garden,
  and like a spring of water, whose waters fail not.
And they that shall be of thee shall build the old waste places:
  thou shalt raise up the foundations of many generations;
and thou shalt be called,
  The repairer of the breach,
  The restorer of paths to dwell in.

If thou turn away thy foot from the sabbath,
  from doing thy pleasure on my holy day;
and call the sabbath a delight,
  the holy of the Lord, honourable;
and shalt honour him, not doing thine own ways,
  nor finding thine own pleasure,
  nor speaking thine own words:
Then shalt thou delight thyself in the Lord;
  and I will cause thee to ride upon the high places of the earth,
and feed thee with the heritage of Jacob thy father:
  for the mouth of the Lord hath spoken it.

JERUSALEM'S GLORIOUS FUTURE
Isaiah 60:1–5, 15–22

Arise, shine; for thy light is come,
  and the glory of the Lord is risen upon thee.

For, behold, the darkness shall cover the earth,
  and gross darkness the people:
but the Lord shall arise upon thee,
  and his glory shall be seen upon thee.
And the Gentiles shall come to thy light,
  and kings to the brightness of thy rising.

Lift up thine eyes round about, and see:
  all they gather themselves together, they come to thee:
thy sons shall come from far,
  and thy daughters shall be nursed at thy side.
Then thou shalt see, and flow together,
  and thine heart shall fear, and be enlarged;
because the abundance of the sea shall be converted unto thee,
  the forces of the Gentiles shall come unto thee...

Whereas thou hast been forsaken and hated,
  so that no man went through thee,
I will make thee an eternal excellency,
  a joy of many generations.
Thou shalt also suck the milk of the Gentiles,
  and shalt suck the breast of kings:
and thou shalt know that I the Lord am thy Saviour
  and thy Redeemer, the mighty One of Jacob.
For brass I will bring gold, and for iron I will bring silver,
  and for wood brass, and for stones iron:
I will also make thy officers peace,
  and thine exactors righteousness.
Violence shall no more be heard in thy land,
  wasting nor destruction within thy borders;
but thou shalt call thy walls Salvation,
  and thy gates Praise.
The sun shall be no more thy light by day;
  neither for brightness shall the moon give light unto thee:
but the Lord shall be unto thee an everlasting light,
  and thy God thy glory.
Thy sun shall no more go down;
  neither shall thy moon withdraw itself:

for the Lord shall be thine everlasting light,
    and the days of thy mourning shall be ended.
Thy people also shall be all righteous:
    they shall inherit the land for ever,
the branch of my planting, the work of my hands,
    that I may be glorified.
A little one shall become a thousand,
    and a small one a strong nation:
I the Lord will hasten it in his time.

THE PROPHET'S MISSION
Isaiah 61:1–3

The Spirit of the Lord God is upon me;
    because the Lord hath anointed me
    to preach good tidings unto the meek;
he hath sent me to bind up the brokenhearted,
    to proclaim liberty to the captives,
    and the opening of the prison to them that are bound;
To proclaim the acceptable year of the Lord,
    and the day of vengeance of our God;
    to comfort all that mourn;
To appoint unto them that mourn in Zion,
    to give unto them beauty for ashes, the oil of joy for mourning,
    the garment of praise for the spirit of heaviness;
that they might be called trees of righteousness,
    the planting of the Lord, that he might be glorified.

THE DAY OF VENGEANCE
Isaiah 63:1–6

Who is this that cometh from Edom,
    with dyed garments from Bozrah?
this that is glorious in his apparel,
    travelling in the greatness of his strength?

I that speak in righteousness,
    mighty to save.
Wherefore art thou red in thine apparel,
    and thy garments like him that treadeth in the winefat?

I have trodden the winepress alone;
    and of the people there was none with me:
for I will tread them in mine anger,
    and trample them in my fury;
and their blood shall be sprinkled upon my garments,
    and I will stain all my raiment.
For the day of vengeance is in mine heart,
    and the year of my redeemed is come.
And I looked, and there was none to help;
    and I wondered that there was none to uphold:
therefore mine own arm brought salvation unto me;
    and my fury, it upheld me.
And I will tread down the people in mine anger,
    and make them drunk in my fury,
and I will bring down their strength to the earth.

A PSALM OF LAMENTATION
Isaiah 63:7 – 64:12

I will mention the lovingkindnesses of the Lord,
    and the praises of the Lord,
according to all that the Lord hath bestowed on us,
    and the great goodness toward the house of Israel,
which he hath bestowed on them according to his mercies,
    and according to the multitude of his lovingkindnesses.
For he said, Surely they are my people, children that will not lie:
    so he was their Saviour.
In all their affliction he was afflicted,
    and the angel of his presence saved them:
in his love and in his pity he redeemed them;
    and he bare them, and carried them all the days of old.

But they rebelled, and vexed his holy Spirit:
>therefore he was turned to be their enemy,
>and he fought against them.
Then he remembered the days of old,
>Moses, and his people,
saying, Where is he that brought them up out of the sea
>with the shepherd of his flock?
>where is he that put his holy Spirit within him?
That led them by the right hand of Moses with his glorious arm,
>dividing the water before them,
>to make himself an everlasting name?
That led them through the deep,
>as an horse in the wilderness,
>that they should not stumble?
As a beast goeth down into the valley,
>the Spirit of the Lord caused him to rest:
so didst thou lead thy people,
>to make thyself a glorious name.

Look down from heaven, and behold
>from the habitation of thy holiness and of thy glory:
where is thy zeal and thy strength,
>the sounding of thy bowels and of thy mercies toward me?
>are they restrained?
Doubtless thou art our father,
>though Abraham be ignorant of us,
>and Israel acknowledge us not:
thou, O Lord, art our father, our redeemer;
>thy name is from everlasting.
O Lord, why hast thou made us to err from thy ways,
>and hardened our heart from thy fear?
Return for thy servants' sake,
>the tribes of thine inheritance.
The people of thy holiness have possessed it but a little while:
>our adversaries have trodden down thy sanctuary.
We are thine: thou never barest rule over them;
>they were not called by thy name.

Oh that thou wouldest rend the heavens,
    that thou wouldest come down,
    that the mountains might flow down at thy presence,
As when the melting fire burneth,
    the fire causeth the waters to boil,
to make thy name known to thine adversaries,
    that the nations may tremble at thy presence!
When thou didst terrible things which we looked not for,
    thou camest down,
    the mountains flowed down at thy presence.
For since the beginning of the world men have not heard,
    nor perceived by the ear,
neither hath the eye seen, O God, beside thee,
    what he hath prepared for him that waiteth for him.
Thou meetest him that rejoiceth
    and worketh righteousness,
    those that remember thee in thy ways:
behold, thou art wroth; for we have sinned:
    in those is continuance, and we shall be saved.
But we are all as an unclean thing,
    and all our righteousnesses are as filthy rags;
and we all do fade as a leaf;
    and our iniquities, like the wind, have taken us away.
And there is none that calleth upon thy name,
    that stirreth up himself to take hold of thee:
for thou hast hid thy face from us,
    and hast consumed us, because of our iniquities.
But now, O Lord, thou art our father;
    we are the clay,
and thou our potter;
    and we all are the work of thy hand.
Be not wroth very sore, O Lord,
    neither remember iniquity for ever:
    behold, see, we beseech thee, we are all thy people.
Thy holy cities are a wilderness,
    Zion is a wilderness,
    Jerusalem a desolation.

Our holy and our beautiful house,
  where our fathers praised thee,
is burned up with fire:
  and all our pleasant things are laid waste.
Wilt thou refrain thyself for these things, O Lord?
  wilt thou hold thy peace, and afflict us very sore?

A REBELLIOUS PEOPLE
Isaiah 65:1–5

I am sought of them that asked not for me;
  I am found of them that sought me not:
I said, Behold me, behold me,
  unto a nation that was not called by my name.
I have spread out my hands all the day
  unto a rebellious people,
which walketh in a way that was not good,
  after their own thoughts;
A people that provoketh me to anger continually to my face;
  that sacrificeth in gardens,
  and burneth incense upon altars of brick;
Which remain among the graves,
  and lodge in the monuments,
which eat swine's flesh,
  and broth of abominable things is in their vessels;
Which say, Stand by thyself, come not near to me;
  for I am holier than thou.
These are a smoke in my nose,
  a fire that burneth all the day.

A NEW HEAVENS AND NEW EARTH
Isaiah 65:17–25

For, behold, I create new heavens and a new earth:
  and the former shall not be remembered,
  nor come into mind.

But be ye glad and rejoice for ever in that which I create:
    for, behold, I create Jerusalem a rejoicing,
    and her people a joy.
And I will rejoice in Jerusalem, and joy in my people:
    and the voice of weeping shall be no more heard in her,
    nor the voice of crying.

There shall be no more thence an infant of days,
    nor an old man that hath not filled his days:
for the child shall die an hundred years old;
    but the sinner being an hundred years old shall be accursed.
And they shall build houses, and inhabit them;
    and they shall plant vineyards,
    and eat the fruit of them.
They shall not build, and another inhabit;
    they shall not plant, and another eat:
for as the days of a tree are the days of my people,
    and mine elect shall long enjoy the work of their hands.
They shall not labour in vain, nor bring forth for trouble;
    for they are the seed of the blessed of the Lord,
    and their offspring with them.
And it shall come to pass, that before they call, I will answer;
    and while they are yet speaking, I will hear.
The wolf and the lamb shall feed together,
    and the lion shall eat straw like the bullock:
    and dust shall be the serpent's meat.
They shall not hurt nor destroy in all my holy mountain,
      saith the Lord.

THE LOVE AND ANGER OF GOD
Isaiah 66:1–2, 12–16, 22–24

Thus saith the Lord,

    The heaven is my throne, and the earth is my footstool:
      where is the house that ye build unto me?
      and where is the place of my rest?

For all those things hath mine hand made,
  and all those things have been,
    saith the Lord:
but to this man will I look,
  even to him that is poor and of a contrite spirit,
  and trembleth at my word...

For thus saith the Lord,

Behold, I will extend peace to her like a river,
  and the glory of the Gentiles like a flowing stream:
then shall ye suck, ye shall be borne upon her sides,
  and be dandled upon her knees.
As one whom his mother comforteth, so will I comfort you;
  and ye shall be comforted in Jerusalem.
And when ye see this, your heart shall rejoice,
  and your bones shall flourish like an herb:
and the hand of the Lord shall be known toward his servants,
  and his indignation toward his enemies.
For, behold, the Lord will come with fire,
  and with his chariots like a whirlwind,
to render his anger with fury,
  and his rebuke with flames of fire.
For by fire and by his sword will the Lord plead with all flesh:
  and the slain of the Lord shall be many...

For as the new heavens and the new earth,
  which I will make, shall remain before me,
    saith the Lord,
so shall your seed and your name remain.
And it shall come to pass, that from one new moon to another,
  and from one sabbath to another,
  shall all flesh come to worship before me,
    saith the Lord.
And they shall go forth, and look upon
  the carcases of the men that have transgressed against me:
for their worm shall not die,
  neither shall their fire be quenched;
  and they shall be an abhorring unto all flesh.

Malachi

GOD CLAIMS HIS HONOUR
Malachi 1:1–3, 6–7, 10–11

The burden of the word of the Lord to Israel by Malachi.

I have loved you, saith the Lord. Yet ye say, Wherein hast thou loved us? Was not Esau Jacob's brother? saith the Lord: yet I loved Jacob, and I hated Esau, and laid his mountains and his heritage waste for the dragons of the wilderness...

A son honoureth his father, and a servant his master: if then I be a father, where is mine honour? and if I be a master, where is my fear? saith the Lord of hosts unto you, O priests, that despise my name. And ye say, Wherein have we despised thy name? Ye offer polluted bread upon mine altar; and ye say, Wherein have we polluted thee? In that ye say, The table of the Lord is contemptible...

Who is there even among you that would shut the doors for nought? neither do ye kindle fire on mine altar for nought. I have no pleasure in you, saith the Lord of hosts, neither will I accept an offering at your hand. For from the rising of the sun even unto the going down of the same my name shall be great among the Gentiles; and in every place incense shall be offered unto my name, and a pure offering: for my name shall be great among the heathen, saith the Lord of hosts.

THE DAY OF THE LORD SHALL COME
Malachi 2:17 – 3:5, 13 – 4:6

Ye have wearied the Lord with your words. Yet ye say, Wherein have we wearied him? When ye say, Every one that doeth evil is good in the sight of the Lord, and he delighteth in them; or, Where is the God of judgment?

Behold, I will send my messenger, and he shall prepare the way before me: and the Lord, whom ye seek, shall suddenly come to his temple, even the messenger of the covenant, whom ye delight in: behold, he shall come, saith the Lord of hosts.

But who may abide the day of his coming? and who shall stand when he appeareth? for he is like a refiner's fire, and like fullers' soap: And he shall sit as a refiner and purifier of silver: and he shall purify the sons of Levi, and purge them as gold and silver, that they may offer unto the Lord an offering in righteousness. Then shall the offering of Judah and Jerusalem be pleasant unto the Lord, as in the days of old, and as in former years.

And I will come near to you to judgment; and I will be a swift witness against the sorcerers, and against the adulterers, and against false swearers, and against those that oppress the hireling in his wages, the widow, and the fatherless, and that turn aside the stranger from his right, and fear not me, saith the Lord of hosts...

Your words have been stout against me, saith the Lord. Yet ye say, What have we spoken so much against thee? Ye have said, It is vain to serve God: and what profit is it that we have kept his ordinance, and that we have walked mournfully before the Lord of hosts? And now we call the proud happy; yea, they that work wickedness are set up; yea, they that tempt God are even delivered.

Then they that feared the Lord spake often one to another: and the Lord hearkened, and heard it, and a book of remembrance was written before him for them that feared the Lord, and that thought upon his name.

And they shall be mine, saith the Lord of hosts, in that day when I make up my jewels; and I will spare them, as a man spareth his own son that serveth him. Then shall ye return, and discern between the righteous and the wicked, between him that serveth God and him that serveth him not.

For, behold, the day cometh, that shall burn as an oven; and all the proud, yea, and all that do wickedly, shall be stubble: and the day that cometh shall burn them up, saith the Lord of hosts, that it shall leave them neither root nor branch. But unto you that fear my name shall the Sun of righteousness arise with healing in his wings; and ye shall go forth, and grow up as calves of the stall. And ye shall tread down the wicked; for they shall be ashes under the soles of your feet in the day that I shall do this, saith the Lord of hosts.

Remember ye the law of Moses my servant, which I commanded unto him in Horeb for all Israel, with the statutes and judgments. Behold, I will send you Elijah the prophet before the coming of the great and dreadful day of the Lord: and he shall turn the heart of the fathers to the children, and the heart of the children to their fathers, lest I come and smite the earth with a curse.

Joel

THE ARMY OF LOCUSTS
Joel 1:1–6, 2:1–11

The word of the Lord that came to Joel the son of Pethuel.

Hear this, ye old men, and give ear,
    all ye inhabitants of the land.
Hath this been in your days,
    or even in the days of your fathers?
Tell ye your children of it,
    and let your children tell their children,
    and their children another generation.
That which the palmerworm hath left
    hath the locust eaten;
and that which the locust hath left
    hath the cankerworm eaten;
and that which the cankerworm hath left
    hath the caterpiller eaten.

Awake, ye drunkards, and weep;
    and howl, all ye drinkers of wine,
because of the new wine;
    for it is cut off from your mouth.
For a nation is come up upon my land,
    strong, and without number,
whose teeth are the teeth of a lion,
    and he hath the cheek teeth of a great lion...

Blow ye the trumpet in Zion,
    and sound an alarm in my holy mountain:
let all the inhabitants of the land tremble:
    for the day of the Lord cometh,
    for it is nigh at hand;

A day of darkness and of gloominess,
    a day of clouds and of thick darkness,
    as the morning spread upon the mountains:
a great people and a strong;
    there hath not been ever the like,
neither shall be any more after it,
    even to the years of many generations.

A fire devoureth before them;
    and behind them a flame burneth:
the land is as the garden of Eden before them,
    and behind them a desolate wilderness;
    yea, and nothing shall escape them.
The appearance of them is as the appearance of horses;
    and as horsemen, so shall they run.
Like the noise of chariots on the tops of mountains
    shall they leap,
like the noise of a flame of fire that devoureth the stubble,
    as a strong people set in battle array.
Before their face the people shall be much pained:
    all faces shall gather blackness.
They shall run like mighty men;
    they shall climb the wall like men of war;
and they shall march every one on his ways,
    and they shall not break their ranks:
Neither shall one thrust another;
    they shall walk every one in his path:
and when they fall upon the sword,
    they shall not be wounded.
They shall run to and fro in the city;
    they shall run upon the wall,
they shall climb up upon the houses;
    they shall enter in at the windows like a thief.
The earth shall quake before them;
    the heavens shall tremble:
the sun and the moon shall be dark,
    and the stars shall withdraw their shining:

And the Lord shall utter his voice before his army:
　　for his camp is very great:
　　for he is strong that executeth his word:
for the day of the Lord is great and very terrible;
　　and who can abide it?

A CALL TO REPENTANCE
Joel 2:12–17

Therefore also now,
　　saith the Lord,
　　turn ye even to me with all your heart,
　　and with fasting, and with weeping, and with mourning:
And rend your heart, and not your garments,
　　and turn unto the Lord your God:
for he is gracious and merciful,
　　slow to anger, and of great kindness,
　　and repenteth him of the evil.
Who knoweth if he will return and repent,
　　and leave a blessing behind him;
even a meat offering and a drink offering
　　unto the Lord your God?

Blow the trumpet in Zion,
　　sanctify a fast, call a solemn assembly:
Gather the people, sanctify the congregation,
　　assemble the elders, gather the children,
　　and those that suck the breasts:
let the bridegroom go forth of his chamber,
　　and the bride out of her closet.
Let the priests, the ministers of the Lord,
　　weep between the porch and the altar,
　　and let them say,
Spare thy people, O Lord,
　　and give not thine heritage to reproach,
　　that the heathen should rule over them:

wherefore should they say among the people,
    Where is their God?

GOD'S PROMISE OF DELIVERANCE
Joel 2:18–32

Then will the Lord be jealous for his land,
    and pity his people.
Yea, the Lord will answer
    and say unto his people,
Behold, I will send you corn, and wine, and oil,
    and ye shall be satisfied therewith:
and I will no more make you a reproach
    among the heathen:
But I will remove far off from you the northern army,
    and will drive him into a land barren and desolate,
with his face toward the east sea,
    and his hinder part toward the utmost sea,
and his stink shall come up,
    and his ill savour shall come up,
because he hath done great things.

Fear not, O land; be glad and rejoice:
    for the Lord will do great things.
Be not afraid, ye beasts of the field:
    for the pastures of the wilderness do spring,
for the tree beareth her fruit,
    the fig tree and the vine do yield their strength.
Be glad then, ye children of Zion,
    and rejoice in the Lord your God:
for he hath given you the former rain moderately,
    and he will cause to come down for you the rain,
the former rain,
    and the latter rain in the first month.
And the floors shall be full of wheat,
    and the vats shall overflow with wine and oil.

And I will restore to you the years that the locust hath eaten,
    the cankerworm, and the caterpiller, and the palmerworm,
    my great army which I sent among you.
And ye shall eat in plenty, and be satisfied,
    and praise the name of the Lord your God,
that hath dealt wondrously with you:
    and my people shall never be ashamed.
And ye shall know that I am in the midst of Israel,
    and that I am the Lord your God, and none else:
    and my people shall never be ashamed.

And it shall come to pass afterward,
    that I will pour out my spirit upon all flesh;
and your sons and your daughters shall prophesy,
    your old men shall dream dreams,
    your young men shall see visions:
And also upon the servants and upon the handmaids
    in those days will I pour out my spirit.
And I will shew wonders in the heavens and in the earth,
    blood, and fire, and pillars of smoke.
The sun shall be turned into darkness,
    and the moon into blood,
    before the great and terrible day of the Lord come.
And it shall come to pass, that whosoever
    shall call on the name of the Lord shall be delivered:
for in mount Zion and in Jerusalem shall be deliverance,
    as the Lord hath said,
and in the remnant
    whom the Lord shall call.

THE FINAL BATTLE
Joel 3:1–3, 7–17

For, behold, in those days, and in that time,
    when I shall bring again the captivity of Judah and Jerusalem,
I will also gather all nations,
    and will bring them down into the valley of Jehoshaphat,

and will plead with them there for my people
    and for my heritage Israel,
whom they have scattered among the nations,
    and parted my land.
And they have cast lots for my people;
    and have given a boy for an harlot,
    and sold a girl for wine, that they might drink...

Behold, I will raise them out of the place whither ye have sold them, and will return your recompence upon your own head: and I will sell your sons and your daughters into the hand of the children of Judah, and they shall sell them to the Sabeans, to a people far off: for the Lord hath spoken it.

Proclaim ye this among the Gentiles;
Prepare war, wake up the mighty men,
    let all the men of war draw near;
    let them come up:
Beat your plowshares into swords
    and your pruninghooks into spears:
    let the weak say, I am strong.
Assemble yourselves, and come, all ye heathen,
    and gather yourselves together round about:
thither cause thy mighty ones to come down, O Lord.

Let the heathen be wakened,
    and come up to the valley of Jehoshaphat:
    for there will I sit to judge all the heathen round about.
Put ye in the sickle, for the harvest is ripe:
    come, get you down;
for the press is full, the fats overflow;
    for their wickedness is great.

Multitudes, multitudes in the valley of decision:
    for the day of the Lord is near in the valley of decision.
The sun and the moon shall be darkened,
    and the stars shall withdraw their shining.
The Lord also shall roar out of Zion,
    and utter his voice from Jerusalem;
    and the heavens and the earth shall shake:

but the Lord will be the hope of his people,
    and the strength of the children of Israel.

So shall ye know that I am the Lord your God
    dwelling in Zion, my holy mountain:
then shall Jerusalem be holy,
    and there shall no strangers pass through her any more.

ISRAEL'S GLORIOUS FUTURE
Joel 3:18–21

And it shall come to pass in that day,
    that the mountains shall drop down new wine,
and the hills shall flow with milk,
    and all the rivers of Judah shall flow with waters,
and a fountain shall come forth out of the house of the Lord,
    and shall water the valley of Shittim.
Egypt shall be a desolation,
    and Edom shall be a desolate wilderness,
for the violence against the children of Judah,
    because they have shed innocent blood in their land.
But Judah shall dwell for ever,
    and Jerusalem from generation to generation.
For I will cleanse their blood that I have not cleansed:
    for the Lord dwelleth in Zion.

Daniel

THE VISION OF THE FOUR BEASTS
Daniel 7:1–8

In the first year of Belshazzar king of Babylon Daniel had a dream and visions of his head upon his bed: then he wrote the dream, and told the sum of the matters.

Daniel spake and said, I saw in my vision by night, and, behold, the four winds of the heaven strove upon the great sea. And four great beasts came up from the sea, diverse one from another.

The first was like a lion, and had eagle's wings: I beheld till the wings thereof were plucked, and it was lifted up from the earth, and made stand upon the feet as a man, and a man's heart was given to it.

And behold another beast, a second, like to a bear, and it raised up itself on one side, and it had three ribs in the mouth of it between the teeth of it: and they said thus unto it, Arise, devour much flesh.

After this I beheld, and lo another, like a leopard, which had upon the back of it four wings of a fowl; the beast had also four heads; and dominion was given to it.

After this I saw in the night visions, and behold a fourth beast, dreadful and terrible, and strong exceedingly; and it had great iron teeth: it devoured and brake in pieces, and stamped the residue with the feet of it: and it was diverse from all the beasts that were before it; and it had ten horns.

I considered the horns, and, behold, there came up among them another little horn, before whom there were three of the first horns plucked up by the roots: and, behold, in this horn were eyes like the eyes of man, and a mouth speaking great things.

THE VISION OF THE ANCIENT OF DAYS
Daniel 7:9–14

I beheld till the thrones were cast down, and the Ancient of days did sit, whose garment was white as snow, and the hair of his head like the pure wool: his throne was like the fiery flame, and his wheels as burning fire. A fiery stream issued and came forth from before him: thousand thousands ministered unto him, and ten thousand times ten thousand stood before him: the judgment was set, and the books were opened.

I beheld then because of the voice of the great words which the horn spake: I beheld even till the beast was slain, and his body destroyed, and given to the burning flame. As concerning the rest of the beasts, they had their dominion taken away: yet their lives were prolonged for a season and time.

I saw in the night visions, and, behold, one like the Son of man came with the clouds of heaven, and came to the Ancient of days, and they brought him near before him. And there was given him dominion, and glory, and a kingdom, that all people, nations, and languages, should serve him: his dominion is an everlasting dominion, which shall not pass away, and his kingdom that which shall not be destroyed.

THE INTERPRETATION OF THE VISIONS
Daniel 7:15–28

I Daniel was grieved in my spirit in the midst of my body, and the visions of my head troubled me. I came near unto one of them that stood by, and asked him the truth of all this. So he told me, and made me know the interpretation of the things.

These great beasts, which are four, are four kings, which shall arise out of the earth. But the saints of the most High shall take the kingdom, and possess the kingdom for ever, even for ever and ever.

Then I would know the truth of the fourth beast, which was diverse from all the others, exceeding dreadful, whose teeth were of iron, and his nails of brass; which devoured, brake in pieces, and stamped the residue with his feet; and of the ten horns that were in his head, and of the other which came up, and before whom three fell; even of that horn that had eyes, and a mouth that spake very great things, whose look was more stout than his fellows.

I beheld, and the same horn made war with the saints, and

prevailed against them; until the Ancient of days came, and judgment was given to the saints of the most High; and the time came that the saints possessed the kingdom.

Thus he said, The fourth beast shall be the fourth kingdom upon earth, which shall be diverse from all kingdoms, and shall devour the whole earth, and shall tread it down, and break it in pieces. And the ten horns out of this kingdom are ten kings that shall arise: and another shall rise after them; and he shall be diverse from the first, and he shall subdue three kings. And he shall speak great words against the most High, and shall wear out the saints of the most High, and think to change times and laws: and they shall be given into his hand until a time and times and the dividing of time.

But the judgment shall sit, and they shall take away his dominion, to consume and to destroy it unto the end. And the kingdom and dominion, and the greatness of the kingdom under the whole heaven, shall be given to the people of the saints of the most High, whose kingdom is an everlasting kingdom, and all dominions shall serve and obey him.

Hitherto is the end of the matter. As for me Daniel, my cogitations much troubled me, and my countenance changed in me: but I kept the matter in my heart.

DANIEL'S PRAYER
Daniel 9:1–19

In the first year of Darius the son of Ahasuerus, of the seed of the Medes, which was made king over the realm of the Chaldeans; in the first year of his reign I Daniel understood by books the number of the years, whereof the word of the Lord came to Jeremiah the prophet, that he would accomplish seventy years in the desolations of Jerusalem.

And I set my face unto the Lord God, to seek by prayer and supplications, with fasting, and sackcloth, and ashes: and I prayed unto the Lord my God, and made my confession, and said,

O Lord, the great and dreadful God, keeping the covenant and mercy to them that love him, and to them that keep his commandments; we have sinned, and have committed iniquity, and have done wickedly, and have rebelled, even by departing from thy precepts and from thy judgments: neither have we hearkened unto thy servants the prophets, which spake in thy name to our kings, our princes, and our fathers, and to all the people of the land.

O Lord, righteousness belongeth unto thee, but unto us confusion of faces, as at this day; to the men of Judah, and to the inhabitants of Jerusalem, and unto all Israel, that are near, and that are far off, through all the countries whither thou hast driven them, because of their trespass that they have trespassed against thee. O Lord, to us belongeth confusion of face, to our kings, to our princes, and to our fathers, because we have sinned against thee. To the Lord our God belong mercies and forgivenesses, though we have rebelled against him; neither have we obeyed the voice of the Lord our God, to walk in his laws, which he set before us by his servants the prophets. Yea, all Israel have transgressed thy law, even by departing, that they might not obey thy voice; therefore the curse is poured upon us, and the oath that is written in the law of Moses the servant of God, because we have sinned against him.

And he hath confirmed his words, which he spake against us, and against our judges that judged us, by bringing upon us a great evil: for under the whole heaven hath not been done as hath been done upon Jerusalem. As it is written in the law of Moses, all this evil is come upon us: yet made we not our prayer before the Lord our God, that we might turn from our iniquities, and understand thy truth. Therefore hath the Lord watched upon the evil, and brought it upon us: for the Lord our God is righteous in all his works which he doeth: for we obeyed not his voice.

And now, O Lord our God, that hast brought thy people forth out of the land of Egypt with a mighty hand, and hast gotten thee renown, as at this day; we have sinned, we have done wickedly. O Lord, according to all thy righteousness, I beseech thee, let thine anger and thy fury be turned away from thy city Jerusalem, thy holy mountain: because for our sins, and for the iniquities of our fathers, Jerusalem and thy people are become a reproach to all that are about us.

Now therefore, O our God, hear the prayer of thy servant, and his supplications, and cause thy face to shine upon thy sanctuary that is desolate, for the Lord's sake. O my God, incline thine ear, and hear; open thine eyes, and behold our desolations, and the city which is called by thy name: for we do not present our supplications before thee for our righteousnesses, but for thy great mercies. O Lord, hear; O Lord, forgive; O Lord, hearken and do; defer not, for thine own sake, O my God: for thy city and thy people are called by thy name.

THE PROPHECY OF THE SEVENTY WEEKS
Daniel 9:20–27

And whiles I was speaking, and praying, and confessing my sin and the sin of my people Israel, and presenting my supplication before the Lord my God for the holy mountain of my God; yea, whiles I was speaking in prayer, even the man Gabriel, whom I had seen in the vision at the beginning, being caused to fly swiftly, touched me about the time of the evening oblation. And he informed me, and talked with me, and said, O Daniel, I am now come forth to give thee skill and understanding. At the beginning of thy supplications the commandment came forth, and I am come to shew thee; for thou art greatly beloved: therefore understand the matter, and consider the vision.

Seventy weeks are determined upon thy people and upon thy holy city, to finish the transgression, and to make an end of sins, and to make reconciliation for iniquity, and to bring in everlasting righteousness, and to seal up the vision and prophecy, and to anoint the most Holy.

Know therefore and understand, that from the going forth of the commandment to restore and to build Jerusalem unto the Messiah the Prince shall be seven weeks, and threescore and two weeks: the street shall be built again, and the wall, even in troublous times. And after threescore and two weeks shall Messiah be cut off, but not for himself: and the people of the prince that shall come shall destroy the city and the sanctuary; and the end thereof shall be with a flood, and unto the end of the war desolations are determined. And he shall confirm the covenant with many for one week: and in the midst of the week he shall cause the sacrifice and the oblation to cease, and for the overspreading of abominations he shall make it desolate, even until the consummation, and that determined shall be poured upon the desolate.

THE VISION OF THE MAN CLOTHED IN LINEN
Daniel 10:1–14

In the third year of Cyrus king of Persia a thing was revealed unto Daniel, whose name was called Belteshazzar; and the thing was true, but the time appointed was long: and he understood the thing, and had understanding of the vision.

In those days I Daniel was mourning three full weeks. I ate no pleasant bread, neither came flesh nor wine in my mouth, neither did I anoint myself at all, till three whole weeks were fulfilled.

And in the four and twentieth day of the first month, as I was by the side of the great river, which is Hiddekel; then I lifted up mine eyes, and looked, and behold a certain man clothed in linen, whose loins were girded with fine gold of Uphaz: his body also was like the beryl, and his face as the appearance of lightning, and his eyes as lamps of fire, and his arms and his feet like in colour to polished brass, and the voice of his words like the voice of a multitude.

And I Daniel alone saw the vision: for the men that were with me saw not the vision; but a great quaking fell upon them, so that they fled to hide themselves. Therefore I was left alone, and saw this great vision, and there remained no strength in me: for my comeliness was turned in me into corruption, and I retained no strength. Yet heard I the voice of his words: and when I heard the voice of his words, then was I in a deep sleep on my face, and my face toward the ground.

And, behold, an hand touched me, which set me upon my knees

and upon the palms of my hands. And he said unto me, O Daniel, a man greatly beloved, understand the words that I speak unto thee, and stand upright: for unto thee am I now sent. And when he had spoken this word unto me, I stood trembling.

Then said he unto me, Fear not, Daniel: for from the first day that thou didst set thine heart to understand, and to chasten thyself before thy God, thy words were heard, and I am come for thy words. But the prince of the kingdom of Persia withstood me one and twenty days: but, lo, Michael, one of the chief princes, came to help me; and I remained there with the kings of Persia. Now I am come to make thee understand what shall befall thy people in the latter days: for yet the vision is for many days.

THE TIME OF THE END
Daniel 12

And at that time shall Michael stand up, the great prince which standeth for the children of thy people: and there shall be a time of trouble, such as never was since there was a nation even to that same time: and at that time thy people shall be delivered, every one that shall be found written in the book. And many of them that sleep in the dust of the earth shall awake, some to everlasting life, and some to shame and everlasting contempt. And they that be wise shall shine as the brightness of the firmament; and they that turn many to righteousness as the stars for ever and ever. But thou, O Daniel, shut up the words, and seal the book, even to the time of the end: many shall run to and fro, and knowledge shall be increased.

Then I Daniel looked, and, behold, there stood other two, the one on this side of the bank of the river, and the other on that side of the bank of the river. And one said to the man clothed in linen, which was upon the waters of the river, How long shall it be to the end of these wonders? And I heard the man clothed in linen, which was upon the waters of the river, when he held up his right hand and his left hand unto heaven, and sware by him that liveth for ever that it shall be for a time, times, and an half; and when he shall have accomplished to scatter the power of the holy people, all these things shall be finished.

And I heard, but I understood not: then said I, O my Lord, what shall be the end of these things?

And he said, Go thy way, Daniel: for the words are closed up and sealed till the time of the end. Many shall be purified, and made white, and tried; but the wicked shall do wickedly: and none of the wicked shall understand; but the wise shall understand.

And from the time that the daily sacrifice shall be taken away, and the abomination that maketh desolate set up, there shall be a thousand two hundred and ninety days. Blessed is he that waiteth, and cometh to the thousand three hundred and five and thirty days.

But go thou thy way till the end be: for thou shalt rest, and stand in thy lot at the end of the days.

Index of Primary Sources